ELUSIVE ELEMENTS
IN PRACTICE

THE LONDON CENTRE FOR PSYCHOTHERAPY

PRACTICE OF PSYCHOTHERAPY SERIES

Series Editors

Bernardine Bishop, Angela Foster,
Josephine Klein, Victoria O'Connell

Book One: Challenges to Practice
Book Two: Ideas in Practice

PRACTICE OF PSYCHOTHERAPY SERIES

BOOK THREE

ELUSIVE ELEMENTS IN PRACTICE

edited by

Bernardine Bishop, Angela Foster,
Josephine Klein, Victoria O'Connell

on behalf of

The London Centre for Psychotherapy

KARNAC

LONDON   NEW YORK

First published in 2004 by
H. Karnac (Books) Ltd.
6 Pembroke Buildings, London NW10 6RE

British Library Cataloguing in Publication Data

A C.I.P. for this book is available from the British Library

ISBN 185575 947 0

10 9 8 7 6 5 4 3 2 1

Designed and typeset by The Studio Publishing Services Ltd, Exeter EX4 8JN

www.karnacbooks.com

CONTENTS

EDITORS AND CONTRIBUTORS

All contributors to this book are members of the London Centre for Psychotherapy

PATRICIA ALLEN trained with the British Association of Psychotherapists in the early 1980s. She is the author of some clinical articles, co-ordinator of, and a seminar leader on, the LCP Infant Observation training and a training psychotherapist. She works in full time private practice.

BERNARDINE BISHOP has a background in academic English, writing and teaching. She is a psychoanalytic psychotherapist in private practice in London.

FAYE CAREY is a psychotherapist in private practice and a principal lecturer in higher education.

NATHAN FIELD is an analytical psychotherapist with over thirty years experience, now retired. He is the author of *Breakdown and breakthrough; Psychotherapy in a new dimension*, Routledge, 1996.

ANGELA FOSTER is a psychoanalytic psychotherapist in private practice, an organizational consultant and a teacher of psychoanalytic organizational consultation at the Tavistock Clinic. She has published widely in the field of mental health and is co-editor of and a principal contributor to *Managing Mental Health in the Community: chaos and containment*. Foster A. & Roberts V. Z. (Eds.), Routledge, 1998.

JOSEPHINE KLEIN was an academic for the first twenty years of her professional life and then a psychoanalytic psychotherapist in private practice, now retired. She has written *Our Need for Others and its Roots in Infancy*, Routledge, previously Tavistock, 1987, *Doubts and Uncertainties in the Practice of Psychotherapy*, Karnac Books, 1995 and *Jacob's Ladder; Essays on experiences of the ineffable in the context of psychotherapy*, Karnac Books, 2003.

STEVEN MENDOZA was a postgraduate student of Human Learning at Brunel University and a generic social worker. He has been a teacher for the London Centre for Psychotherapy and other trainings and has worked full time in private practice since 1982. He is the author of 'Genital and phallic homosexuality' published in *Sexuality: Psychoanalytic Perspectives*, Harding, C. (Ed). Brunner Routledge, 2001.

VICTORIA O'CONNELL comes from a background of work with children with emotional difficulties. She is now a psychoanalytic psychotherapist in private practice.

The London Centre for Psychotherapy

The London Centre for Psychotherapy has its origins in the 1950s and became a registered charity in 1974. Its activities are threefold:

- To offer training in psychoanalytic psychotherapy (including analytical psychology) in which the leading schools of analytic thought and practice are represented,
- To organise post-graduate professional activities, and,
- To provide a psychotherapy service to the community through its clinic.

The Centre is the professional association of around 200 practising psychotherapists who are registered, through the Centre, with the British Confederation of Psychotherapists.

The LCP

32 Leighton Road ● Kentish Town ● London NW5 2QE
Telephone: 020 7482 2002/2282 ● Fax: 020 7482 4222

www.lcp-psychotherapy.org.uk

Registered Charity No. 267244

Introduction

Josephine Klein

The editors had trouble finding an appropriate title for this volume in the LCP series **The Practice of Psychotherapy**. It was hard to find words that were accurate, descriptive and un-embarrassing. *Elusive Elements in Practice* was the best we found, to follow the previous *Challenges to Practice* and *Ideas in Practice*. For a while we played with "On the Margins of Practice" but that did not feel sufficiently informative; "The Ineffable in Practice" brought in too unfamiliar a word; jokingly we talked of the imponderable in practice. "Eccentric" would have given the wrong impression because the word now means primarily "peculiar" but, deriving it from ex-centric, *The Shorter Oxford English Dictionary* still gives primacy to the meaning of "not centrally placed", "being abnormally centred", and this exactly describes a common element in these papers. These more or less eccentric papers manifest more or less bold departures from commonly received wisdom. To that extent they may help extend the frontiers of some concept or of some organized structure of concepts that we call "theory". Commonly accepted theories form the centre of what we practise and teach.

Psychoanalytically-based psychotherapy has quite an extensive central area. And however much we in the central area may quarrel

1

about our central ideas, we tend to agree on what is just too eccentric and is to be regarded with reserve and suspicion. These ideas are left on the margins and, getting less attention, they are more elusive. They will not get concentrated consideration either in the consulting-room or in the study. This is one reason why they are more elusive. But such neglect may cause potentially good ideas to be lost, as well as ridiculous ones. Some potentially valuable ideas are given space in the present volume, *Elusive Elements in Practice*.

It seems desirable to the enquiring mind to bring as much knowledge as possible into a single, comprehensive, conceptual structure. We have interesting records from the Dark and Middle Ages, some of whose best minds tried to reconcile music, mathematics, astrology, astronomy, theology, architecture, and assorted trimmings, into one coherent field-theory. They did not do so badly either: for instance it is only in the recently past century that our ears became free from what we experienced as the proper natural interval between the notes on a scale. In matters of the mind, too, there are those who attempt to weld all the different ways in which we experience aspects of our life into one coherent structure of ideas. Freud tried. Jung tried more comprehensively. Nathan Field in the present volume offers suggestions towards unification, starting from some reflections on the nature and boundaries of what many call "the self".

Field starts with Freud's well-known dictum that the goal of psychoanalysis is to effect a shift from the dominance of the Id to the dominance of the Ego. Field considers this a shift from two-dimensional functioning to three-dimensional functioning. Building on this idea, he now explores the shift from three-dimensional to four-dimensional functioning, a shift he sees as from Ego to Self. This hypothesis about four-dimensional functioning is Field's way of paying attention to the fact that we appear sometimes to affect one another in ways not directly attributable to words and body language. Field includes not only the interpersonal experiences of identification and projective identification, but also what may have been described as "peak experiences", as "connectedness", as "I-Thou" relating, as mystical and, also, as manic delusion—all these may find their proper place in four-dimensional functioning. These rather amorphous-seeming epiphets, whose common factor has something to do with hard-to-account-for experiences of relatedness, are surrounded by an aura of unpredict-ability, lack of logic, weirdness, and other undesirable qualities, and have in recent years attracted some cautious attention from our profession as shown by the appearance of the present volume, with its ample bibliographical references. This attention—and this caution—may be thought a good thing. Why should this area of human experiences be left to anthropologists and cranks? It needs tidying, in our terms as well as theirs. And until it is tidier, much nonsense will inevitably be intertwined with what will turn into good, acceptable sense.

In the later part of his paper, Field briefly discusses his experi-ence of "Christianne", who seemed to him to be functioning in the fourth dimension rather more than most patients. We must honour Field for not blandly ignoring her sometimes odd remarks, and for not interpreting them to her in an obvious, conventional way, though in this paper he reproaches himself, after the event, for lack of imagination in not responding more thoughtfully and in greater depth to her repeated conviction that there was a deep twin-like bond between them from the moment they met. What he had "understood as transference illusion, was more likely the manifes-tation of an archetypal connection with a profound healing poten-tial which I never fully tapped". That is one way of putting it. No doubt there are others, but what matters is

(1) Is this way of putting into words what was felt in this inter-personal event of benefit to the patient and, if so, how?
(2) Is this way better than some other way of describing the event and if so, how?
(3) How can our different insights be put together compatibly?

While Field may be seen as a Jungian of the old school, Patricia Allen's debt to Jungian thought comes at least equally from more recent sources influenced by Fordham (1989), of course, and, with major consequences, by Meltzer and Harris Williams' (1988) *Appre-hension of Beauty*. Allen seeks to explore the reaction evoked in many people by what they experience as beautiful—a reaction which seems increasingly to be called "the aesthetic experience". Following Meltzer and Harris Williams (1988 and elsewhere), she connects these reactions to experiences of a mutually adoring gaze between mother and child in the earliest moments of infancy—an experience also given great importance by both Bernardine Bishop and Jennifer Silverstone in Book Two of the present series, *Ideas in Practice*.

Allen quotes with approval the reference to Jung's (1958) *numinosum* in Proner's (1986) discussion of Meltzer's ideas on the apprehension of beauty and the aesthetic experience, which also gathers into this area of thought those interested in religion, mysticism, and what may be a spiritual dimension. But Allen encourages us to explore these processes in the interaction between patients and analysts, both in their enjoyable, positive forms, and in the distressing variants brought about when hate, envy, or fear of loss have the upper hand and operate to deny, distort, and destroy the impulse to adore and respond to adoration.

Like other semi-explanatory notions in our field, the concept of "aesthetic experience" has an elusive, ambiguous status, sometimes used in discussion as an explanatory myth, sometimes used as an actual factual historical event at the start of life. And indeed, it may be that where something of the sort is entirely lacking, we find the quasi-medical diagnosis of "failure to thrive".

The use of the concept of "aesthetic experience", which has its roots in a hypothetical event in early ineffable moments, does away with the concept of a fourth dimension by incorporating certain experiences into the three dimensions we are used to. There is then no mystery of the kind that captured the imagination of Jung and Field. Fair enough. But it is not immediately obvious to common sense or experience of life that those most alive to beauty were also most privileged in respect of the mutual adoring gaze of mother and infant. However, one great merit of this theory is that it is empirically verifiable. Will someone volunteer? Without verification all theories are equal.

Mendoza is also gripped by the current interest in the idealized mother and child or, rather, by the development of this idea into the concept of the idealized parental couple. Following Bion, Mendoza stretches the language we use to think about internal objects as far as it can be stretched, to allow it to be used for the discussion of our beliefs and feelings as though these are "objects". This is useful if we want to circumvent the common and otherwise apparently inescapable epistemological puzzle that interests some writers in this area: did God create us, or did we create God? Internal objects are allowed to be both "me" and "not-me", and Mendoza considers God to be an internal object of this kind.

Mendoza's reading of Bion and Meltzer takes their ideas to the most elusive extreme that this volume can stand. With Mendoza, more than with the other contributors to this volume, the orderly sequences of logic and syntax are disrupted by the task of expressing the elusive inexpressible—a feature of mysticism that has irritated the tidy-minded throughout the centuries. In a paper packed with unusual ideas derived not only from Bion and Meltzer but also from less well-known sources, Mendoza plaits together a number of current ideas in a way that gives us something of the fascinated, bemused thrill that must have been felt by nineteenth-century scientists and philosophers when Freud's ideas about unconscious processes first met their astonished eyes.

Because the word "atonement" has the double meaning of union (at-one-ment) and of expiation of guilt, Mendoza is able to relate what it means to Melanie Klein's "depressive position".

> The essence of the depressive position is that we can bear to find a good object inside us, that object being the mother or, in a more infantile state, the breast. But to call it mother or breast is to impute to it a meta-psychological nature. The meta-psychological form contains and gives shape to what we might not otherwise be able to delineate. The experience is actual and may be of something both inside and outside. It may not be the self but, for an adult, it is not usually Mummy either. Similarly, religion attributes to this experience a presence of God.

Like Bion, and like Meltzer, Mendoza then equates—or at least associates—this internalized good object with God, with a stage on the path to God by a gradual develpmental process that Josephine Klein (see below) calls a "bootstrap theory". Mendoza quotes Meltzer to the effect that "the best aspect of the mind is beyond self, and the self must evolve in its relation to its internal objects . . ." so that "eventually the most evolved part of an individual's mind lies beyond the experience of self and is apprehended as object". This object, we are allowed to infer, is God, and indeed Mendoza quotes without comment Meltzer's excited claim that "a new proof of the existence of God has evolved most unexpectedly".

Mendoza's paper builds up from Bion, who maintained that, just as we may experience ourselves remembering something we wanted to have happened although it did not in fact happen, so we may also remember something that did happen, but remember it so faultily that we consider it a delusion (because of the extent to which it has been distorted by faulty adhesions). On this basis Bion builds the hypotheses that we may remember an encounter with God—"or O as I have called it to avoid involvement with existing association"—which is so distorted by memories and desires that do not belong to the encounter that we think the experience hallucinatory.

Mendoza's apprehension of the elusive inexpressible world is deeply influenced by insights derived from his Buddhist reading and meditation. In his understanding of the experiences involved, both the process of psychoanalysis at its most searching and profound and the processes of Buddhist discipline reach the same state of mind, which Mendoza relates to, and perhaps equates with, Bion's O and the Buddhist "refuge", of which "the point is always to relinquish the narcissistic, egocentric organization, and to acknowledge the need for something greater then the self"—a theme pursued from a different standpoint by Josephine Klein in the final chapter of this volume

Faye Carey, like Nathan Field, focuses more directly on the fascinating problem of describing what happens between people in moments of relatedness. An artist in the visual world as well as a psychotherapist, her understanding of what can happen at times of relatedness is in terms of the artist's subjective experience of creative episodes. Creativity is another of those as yet shadowy topics that has been glanced at in the last century without gaining a central place in psychotherapeutic thought. Like Patricia Allen, Carey sees creativity happening in the consulting room between patient and therapist in a way that elucidates what happens at those moments. And what happens in the consulting room can never be thought ex-centric to the practice of psychotherapy.

It is interesting that Carey's exploration of creativity uses an idea of a "bootstrap process" very like Mendoza's. A bootstrap process is different from development in that in development the potential of a thing gradually unfolds according to its nature—the pea becomes a pea-plant, the puppy a dog, etc. A bootstrap process is one in which at each stage some kind of assent or effort or input is necessary; some extraneous event, which enables development to move to a level that is not only more complex but more like a new creation.

This creation then has potential for further development, which, however, may again be contingent on new input. Getting through a progressively stiffer set of exams would be like that. Carey hypothesizes a bootstrap process by means of which the infant's interest in the external world is shaped in specific ways by the anxieties aroused during successive conflicts between love-cathexes and hate-cathexes to the mother's body.

Carey addresses the genesis of the creative process from this brave innovatory angle. Giving due respect to Melanie Klein's attribution of creativity to the need for reparative work after guilt, Carey considers quite other sources of creativity. For her, people may engage in creative endeavour *fundamentally*, because it gives them pleasure of a unique kind. This leads her to consider the satisfaction that comes from discovering pleasing forms and meanings, and from the disappearance of previously mismanaged boundaries between self and others, as well as from the cooperative creation of pleasing forms and meanings.

Moreover, there are similarities between what happens in artists' workshops and in psychotherapists' consulting rooms: new conceptual entities come into being in the encounters between patients and their therapists as they do in the encounters between artists and their materials, entities provoked but also limited by the nature of each. This must surely also be what Winnicott had in mind when he allowed his notion of transitional space to spill over into that of cultural space. It may also be a way of describing what Ogden sees as the creation of the intersubjective, analytic third.

Josephine Klein's paper does not wrestle with abstractions. Having noticed that narcissism is not a modern phenomenon, but one that has plagued the Western world for at least a millennium, she looks at its descriptions over the centuries and at the cures that have been variously recommended. Can anything be learned from common factors and contrasting perspectives, if we find any, given that the theories of human interrelatedness on which they are based are so different? Drawing on various Western Christian writers, she identifies two main recommendations. You can concentrate on exterminating self-love and self-interest. Alternatively, you can refuse to concentrate on the self at all: you concentrate on other objects instead—maybe other people, or maybe that huge object, God; either can be so interesting that you simply forget to think about yourself for a while.

She suggests some interesting parallels. There is the parallel between the self-absorption of holiness-seeking people thinking about their sinfulness, and the self-absorption of the narcissistically inclined, whose self-doubt vitiates their useful endeavours. There is the hidden—and occasionally florid—arrogance with which some saints and some patients devalue those with whom they have dealings. There is also a parallel between the way some of the quieter saints developed and the progress of some narcissistically inclined patients helped out of their affliction by a psychotherapist who attended steadily to the possibility of good feelings growing between patient and the therapist and others.

All the contributors to this volume refer at least in passing to events in the consulting-room, and it may be that no general theory (if indeed there can be such a thing) can work if it is not interwoven with empirical considerations from the start. It is possible that only by looking at what we do with ever-fresh eyes—eschewing case-presentations that do nothing but revalidate some generally-accepted notion—that a comprehensive theory can evolve to include some of the events that as yet seem so elusive to us.

> Know then thyself; presume not God to scan,
> The proper study of mankind is man.
>
> [Alexander Pope 1688–1744 An Essay on Man]

or in more modern idiom—

> Best not to theorise about God's features,
> But study our own ways, and other creatures.

Mechanisms and mysteries

Nathan Field

When my patient John first came to see me he was depressed, confused and virtually at the end of his tether. He had not expected to feel so deeply upset when his father died some months earlier. He had fallen out with him many years before, quite unable to forgive him for what he felt was a lifetime of harshness and intimidation. He had barely spoken to him even at his mother's funeral. From his teens onward John had thought of his father as a brute, he saw himself as his victim, and his mother as a martyr. What frightened him now was his unexpected grief at his father's death.

In the therapy, because I was more or less his father's age, he transferred onto me his fear and hatred of male authority figures. I worked hard to sustain an empathic attitude and interpret as helpfully as I could; but he remained deeply mistrustful and interpretations never seemed to sink in. Even though he didn't explicitly reject them, I suspected that they ran off him like rain off plate glass.

The label I might apply to John is "paranoid–schizoid": the paranoia refers to his underlying fear and suspicion; the schizoid means split. By dying his father had become a good object, and I a bad one. John tended to see most of his life in terms of opposites. Usually the opposites did not meet; they just co-existed, like heads on one side of a coin and tails on the other, and John could only believe in the side which was uppermost. Most people who come for therapy function at a similar level. In their judgments they switch from black to white, friend to foe, love to hate, pain to pleasure. Each state of mind, while it persists, totally defines their reality, then flips to its opposite, and carries the same conviction. Like a coin, there is no space for anything in between, namely thought. They live in what I would call the realm of the two-dimensional. I use this term to convey that their perceptions are distorted, rather in the way that large continents are distorted on a map as compared to a globe, and it is little wonder their lives feel existentially flat.

Given John's prevailing hostility towards me, it was a matter of astonishment that he came in one day and said, "I want to thank you for the last session." It was extraordinary to be thanked by him, but I also felt puzzled, because I could hardly even remember what the last session had been about. Cautiously I responded, "What did I say? . . . Perhaps you can remind me." He replied: "It was nothing you said." I became even more confused. He went on, "Do you remember my telling you how I felt when my father made that awful remark . . .?

"Yes, I remember it now."

"Well, I looked at you and saw that you had gone as white as a sheet."

"I did?" Even as he spoke I recalled that lurch of cold despair as I took in how wounded he must have felt.

He said, "For a moment I thought you had come over ill. Then I realized that you knew exactly what I felt at the time. It suddenly sunk in that what happened to me really mattered to you."

There was no need to reply. I knew he was telling me that it had been a transformative moment. That was certainly John's impression, and it turned out to have a lasting effect. From that time forward his mistrust seemed to diminish, his presence became less oppressive, and he even began to think over some of things I said. The interesting thing was that I didn't know at the time that my reaction had been so visible, nor could I have anticipated the impact it would have.

This episode illustrates what, in the language of contemporary psychoanalysis, may be called "non-interpretative mechanisms".

This is the title of a recent paper by Daniel Stern and his colleagues. (Stern, 1998) In it, the authors focus on the therapeutic value of what they term "moments of meeting" between mothers and babies, which they regard as crucial to the natural development of infants. The analytic inference is that the "moment of meeting" may be paralleled in the experience of patients with their therapists.

Stern's group displays a psychoanalytic attitude, currently growing in influence, that places as great a therapeutic value on relationship as on interpretation. Among the earlier advocates of this approach was Harold Searles. He called this very earliest developmental stage "pre-ambivalent symbiosis", by which he meant a state of primary fusion between a loving mother and her infant. He explicitly regarded the chance to live it through in the therapy as vital to basic change. (Searles, 1965) Margaret Little meant the same thing by her term "primary undifferentiation" (Little, 1986). Balint spoke of patient and therapist merging into a "harmonious interpenetrating mix up" which may develop into a decisive "new beginning" for the patient. (Balint, 1968) In John's case our unwitting "moment of meeting" provided the indispensable basis of trust that enabled my interpretations to actually be heard.

It is worth noting that even progressive psychoanalysts like Stern and his group feel obliged to speak of mechanisms, whereas I wish to suggest that they are speaking of mysteries. The simple recognition by my patient John that he really mattered to me initiated a mysterious healing leap to a new level of functioning. In Kleinian terms he made a shift from the paranoid–schizoid position to the depressive. Expressed in my more abstract terminology, he took a step from the second into the third dimension.

A spectrum of mental functioning

The priceless benefit that three-dimensional functioning provides hardly needs emphasizing. It is the goal of psychoanalysis, aptly summarized by Freud when he declared: "Where Id was, let Ego be." Freud, with characteristic irony, expressed it as a shift: "from neurotic misery to common human unhappiness". Nonetheless, it is hardly possible to overestimate what it means to make the transition from neurosis to some sustainable degree of normality, to the achievement of a functioning personality motivated, as Freud expressed it, by "love and work". There is little doubt that this transition is massively facilitated by psychoanalytic interpretation. Interpretation makes sense of our lives by linking our present with our past, our conscious life with the unconscious, our thoughts with our feelings. By inviting us to *think*, rather than merely reacting, it challenges us to look at how we conspire in the creation of our own unhappiness, instead of invariably attributing our problems to everyone and everything around us. To achieve what Freud sought; the dominance of the Ego over the Id is nothing less than waking up to a different kind of reality.

Is it feasible to ask if psychotherapy can take us beyond the Ego? Is "common human unhappiness" the limit of human potential? In what follows I want to explore the possibility of a further shift from Ego to Self. In the terminology I adopt here, this would require a shift from the third to a fourth dimension.

The direct experience of the four-dimensional may be brief and may happen only rarely, but many people have known it some time in their lives. In recent polls in the United States one person in three acknowledged they had had at least one such awakening. These "peak" experiences can be the outcome of consistent prayer or meditation or, a piece of music, a painting, or a line of poetry may spontaneously trigger them. They can happen when our spirit is suddenly uplifted by the infinite expanse of the night sky, or we glimpse what Blake meant when he claimed to "see the World in a grain of sand". It can take place when we are alone or in the company of another, most commonly when we fall in love, or in the act of love, or at the birth of a child.

And it can also occur in the therapy session. At such moments we feel powerfully connected to the other person, yet feel with equal power our own separate selves. I recall it once happened to me in a therapy group. As I looked round the room, each member suddenly appeared to me as their unique self in a way I had never seen before—and that included a sense of my own uniqueness—while at the same time I knew we were all indissolubly connected. On reflection I came to understand it as a spontaneous four-dimensional joining of self and other, analogous to the vision whereby Einstein joined time and space into a four-dimensional "space–time" continuum. Permeating the whole experience was the inexplicable conviction that, in spite of everything, in spite of all the pain and horror in the world, everything everywhere was all right. I glimpsed all this in a single moment of connectedness. Throughout history many people have recorded similar unforgettable moments. Martin Buber would have called it an "I–Thou" experience. The Buddhist tradition uses a less personal word like "suchness." If only for the briefest of moments I became, as one Zen master put it: "vacant and spiritual, empty and marvellous."

It would be possible to pathologize my experience by regarding it as manic delusion. In fact such transcendent glimpses do often occur to certain individuals before or during schizophrenic breakdown. But they also happen to people who remain reasonably sane, and indeed become saner as a result. These glimpses of an altogether deeper reality frequently serve to resolve what seems to the individual at the time to be an insoluble crisis, and lifts them onto an enhanced level of being. They happen even more frequently to those who develop into what could be called super-sane. I am referring to those spiritually trained and gifted individuals, the religious mystics. However, even though untold thousands of people may recall such an experience when questioned, the vast majority simply choose to forget them and continue with their lives unchanged.

I am arguing that these four-dimensional glimpses reveal a level of existence, which we know, at the moment it happens, to be incomparably more *real* than our everyday experience. From the perspective of the fourth dimension our "normal" three-dimensional reality is seen to be a flat, distorted state, what the Eastern religions call "*maya*", or what Bion described as "the trance of everyday life". Physicists like David Bohm would seriously argue that, from the evidence of quantum mechanics and the close study of sub-atomic particles, our solid-seeming, everyday world could be regarded as a form of holographic imagery, a time-bound, inferior facsimile of a timeless reality that we can apprehend but not describe. This timeless reality he called the "Implicate Order" (Bohm, 1982). To the extent that we realize this to be actually the case, we can at least entertain the possibility of waking up out of the third into the fourth dimension, a process that I suggest is parallel to that of my patient John who woke up out of the second dimension into the third.

I have spoken so far of two-, three- and four-dimensionality. What has happened to the one-dimensional? I want to look more closely at this level of normal human functioning, because it has profound bearing on four-dimensional experience. One-dimensionality broadly conforms to Freud's view of the Id, not far removed from the level of animal consciousness, itself dominated by the twin instincts of survival and procreation. In recent years observation of the earliest weeks and months of the normal human infant reveals a more detailed picture. Donald Meltzer says new-born infants occupy "a one-dimensional world", which he describes as

> substantially mindless, consisting of a series of events not available for memory or thought ... Gratification and fusion with the object would be undifferentiated. [Meltzer, 1975]

Frances Tustin (1982), also speaking of normal infants, noted "that earliest infancy seems to be a world of sensations experienced in a fluid way." In the case of autistic children she suggests that

> After birth, sensations of being in a watery medium appear to linger on ... [leaving them with] nameless terrors which arise from the sense of fluidity which permeated their being ... they are afraid of being spilled and flowing away into nothingness. [Tustin, 1982]

The analyst Ogden, drawing on the work of Tustin, Meltzer, Bick, Winnicott, Stern, and others, has proposed a position prior to Melanie Klein's paranoid–schizoid position, which he calls "autistic–contiguous". In this mode

> psychic organisation is derived in large part from sensory contiguity, that is, connections are established through the experience of sensory surfaces "touching" one another ... [This] ... is certainly not a relationship between subjects, as in the depressive mode, nor is it a relationship between objects, as in the paranoid–schizoid mode. ... there is practically no sense of inside or outside, self and other; rather what is important is the pattern, boundedness, shape, rhythm, texture, hardness, softness, warmth, coldness and so on. [Ogden, 1992, p. 31]

This identification of a level of functioning prior to the "paranoid–schizoid" constitutes an important addition to our understanding. But there is a characteristic of one-dimensional experience, which I think Ogden misses, and that is its numinosity. In his book *The Apprehension of Beauty* Meltzer (1988) speculates that the normal, new-born infant is "blinded" by the beauty of its mother's face and breast. Psychoanalysts of an earlier generation, Franz Alexander, for example, attributed a state of bliss to the intra-uterine condition, and identified it with the ecstasy of the mystic (Alexander, 1931). There is undoubtedly a profound resonance between this infantile "blinding", and the frequent reports of blinding or heat in mystical experience. Can we account for the transforming vision of the mature mystic, such as the "dazzling darkness" of Dionysus the Aereopagite, or the inner "fire" of Pascal, by the hypothesis that the primitive numinosity of the first dimension and the meaningfulness of the fourth dimension have become incandescently fused?

It may be timely at this juncture to summarize the essence of the four states I have so far outlined:

the aim of the *one-dimensional* is survival, yet includes the capacity for numinous experience;

the aim of the *second dimension* is gratification, yet shows the rudiments of thinking if only to achieve pleasure;

the aim of the *third dimension* is happiness, which involves the capacity to defer pleasure, but reaches towards a rational and fulfilled life of love and work;

the aim of the *fourth dimension* is meaning, which may involve the sacrifice of happiness, the capacity to learn from and transcend suffering, and to integrate our conflicting desires for both separateness and togetherness.

Each of these successive stages, from the first to the fourth, is innate in human nature, each encompasses its predecessor, and each shift to the next level feels like waking to a new reality.

Analytic explorations in the fourth dimension

To further our understanding we need to consider Jung's unique contribution to our subject. Jung, like Freud, feared the power of the

Unconscious but he also revered it: "The only events in my life worth telling," he said, "are those where the imperishable world irrupted into this transitory one." (Jung, 1971, p. 18). Jung's view of the Unconscious is very different from Freud's. It embraces not only Freud's primitive, yet timeless, Id, but also the whole psychic and spiritual inheritance of mankind, which he called the "archetypes of the collective unconscious". But while it is an immeasurably larger concept, it does raise some conceptual difficulties. By conflating these two poles of the archetypal spectrum, the primitive and the sublime, Jung commits what Ken Wilber calls the "pre-trans fallacy". Wilber argues

> ... since both pre-rational and trans-rational are non-rational, they are easily confused. And then one of two very unpleasant things happens: either you reduce genuine, trans-rational spiritual realities into infantile pre-rational states; or you elevate childish, pre-rational sentiments to transcendental glory. [Wilber, 1998, p. 5]

Although Wilber makes a valid point in insisting that the numinosity of the one-dimensional does not make it the equivalent of the four-dimensional, it must certainly be a vital ingredient in it.

In his paper "Problems of Modern Psychotherapy" (1954, para. 114), Jung presented the therapeutic experience as involving four main processes. The first, confession, refers to the basic need every patient has to feel heard, understood, and not judged. This primary attitude of listening and attunement, of being alongside the patient in a contiguous way, could be regarded working *one-dimensionally*. The second process, education, Jung saw as the main contribution of Adlerian psychology. It meant learning how to live rationally. Adler, once famous, is now little remembered, but his approach has become the central ingredient of the cognitive–analytic method. I would regard it as *working two-dimensionally*. The third process, which Jung called elucidation, is the principal tool of Freudian psychoanalysis and is universally known as interpretation. Its aim is to develop a viable ego and thereby make a shift from the pursuit of pleasure to the pursuit of happiness. I suggest it occupies the *three-dimensional* level. Having introduced these three aspects of the psychotherapeutic experience, Jung then introduces a fourth process, which he calls transformation.

I think he used the word transformation to suggest something unique to his own approach, something that proceeds not through mechanisms but through mysteries; a process that aims not simply to fulfil one's personal potential or to develop satisfying human relationships, but something as yet unknown. Jungian transformation seeks to achieve the further shift from the third to the fourth dimension: in Jung's terms, from the ego complex to the archetype of the Self.

Jung took the view that the activation of an archetype took us into a different order of reality where synchronous and paranormal events may occur. He wrote:

> when an archetype appears it manifests a distinctly numinous character which can only be described as "spiritual", if magical is too strong a word. . . . There is a mystical aura about its numinosity . . . the experience brings with it a depth and fullness of meaning that was unthinkable before. [Jung, 1960, para. 405]

Many psychotherapists have observed such phenomena in their work. Repeatedly I have found that patients who are deeply involved in the therapeutic relationship just happen to know what is on my mind. There are references to it in Balint; and there is also a collection of papers (Devereaux, 1953) on the subject, including some by Freud himself. In it, several psychoanalysts report that their patients had dreamt of actual happenings in their analyst's private life, events of which they could have known nothing. But generally psychoanalysis regards the occult as a taboo subject, and the psychoanalytic literature that addresses the topic is rather sparse.

Unconscious communications occurred more than once in my work with a patient I shall call Christianne. She came from a severely dysfunctional family: her mother was illiterate and prone to paranoid breakdowns; her father was alcoholic and violent to his wife when he was drunk. On one occasion in her childhood, Christianne actually stabbed her father in his shoulder to stop him throttling her mother in a drunken rage. Christianne left home in her late teens and later became an alcoholic herself. Her deterioration culminated in her contracting meningitis, and for a time she lay near death. With recovery her life changed; she stopped drinking and trained as a nurse.

As may happen with some victims of childhood trauma, Christianne developed unusual abilities. I think it also likely that her serious illness may have contributed to what seemed an almost paranormal sensitivity. Survival from a life-threatening illness or accident is quite common in the history of those who develop healing abilities, including the gift of second sight. Christianne told me that, when I opened the door to her for the very first time, she *knew* she had always known me. This grew into the conviction that she and I had been twins in an earlier incarnation. From my analytic standpoint these ideas were all too obviously idealized transference delusions, born out of her need for a loving parent, and what I saw as her fragile grip on reality. I was careful not to puncture these fantasies, but equally careful not to collude with them.

However, some months later Christianne reported, with much concern, an hallucinatory image of me that suddenly appeared to her while at home. She said she could see me sitting up in a hospital bed with a tube emerging from my nose. She feared it meant that I would have to undergo surgery in the near future. From her description I recognized immediately what she described. On this occasion it seemed appropriate to assure her that what she had "seen" and thought was going to happen, had *already* happened to me some years before. The fact that this image of an actual event in my life, of which she knew nothing, had spontaneously come into her mind quite shook my former incredulity and led me to question my sceptical attitude.

With hindsight I see that, although Christianne did get considerable benefit from our work together, at some point I failed her. I now believe I failed to meet her in the numinosity of the therapeutic relationship; failed to see that her strange intuition of a brother–sister bond emanated from a deeper and more spiritual level created by our shared unconscious. What I interpreted as transference illusion was more likely to have been the manifestation of an archetypal connection with a profound healing potential that I never fully tapped.

Perhaps the commonest form of shared unconscious knowledge, reported by a significant number of therapists, presents itself as a somatized counter-transference. That is to say, the therapist experiences unexpected physical sensations that turn out to "belong" to the patient. In my own experience I have been overcome by sudden drowsiness, trembling, tears, stabbing pains in the head, or even sexual arousal, when nothing in the patient's manner or material offered any hint of it. In practice, and depending on circumstances, I may choose to acknowledge these bodily reactions in order to explore them. They usually turn out to represent deeply repressed feelings in my patient that have been split off and projected into me. At the same time I suspect that my own unresolved repressions render me susceptible to these bodily innervations.

What Stern called "moments of meeting" often carry a charge of numinosity in an atmosphere that is intensely intimate yet strangely impersonal. It is as if these moments lie beyond the merely personal. They seem to come out of silence, or an atmosphere, a look, or a spontaneous gesture. But equally they may be conveyed through an interpretation that is not just a correct verbal formulation but also an utterance from the therapist's inner life. This is finely conveyed in the way that Christopher Bollas describes his use of the counter-transference.

> By cultivating a freely-roused emotional sensibility, the analyst welcomes news from within himself that is reported through his own intuitions, feelings, passing images, phantasies and imagined interpretive interventions. . . . In order to find the patient we must look for him within ourselves. [Bollas, 1987, p. 201]

Although I earlier referred to "peak" moments of rapport taking place in the therapy session, equally often I may find myself plunged into "chasmic" states of barely describable disconnection. Within moments of the patient entering the room, I may find myself reduced to a cold, trance-like condition where I cannot think, cannot talk, and feel only the torment of paralysed helplessness. The more I fight it, the worse it gets. It is as if the patient is forcing me to live out every last ounce of his or her despair. Sometimes I simply say aloud what we both know is happening and, by making the situation explicit, struggle to regain a human connection. At other times I have learned that, if I can find the courage simply to give myself up to the frozen emptiness, to suffer it through with the patient in silence, it somehow changes by itself. The deathly chill turns into warmth and the space that formerly divided us now joins us. We may even "sleep together", that is, we may both literally doze off. When, in a little while, we awaken there is a palpable sense of connection; our thoughts flow freely, and a productive, dialogue usually follows. It is as if we had to pass through a breakdown to emerge into a breakthrough. It may be necessary to go through the same process very many times for the negative energy to spend itself. For a deep transformation to take place both the negative and the positive interactions—the shared dying and the shared living—have to be experienced.

As my references to Bollas, Winnicott, Searles, Balint and other psychoanalysts make clear, it would be seriously misleading to attribute to Jung and the post-Jungians a monopoly of the four-dimensional domain. Contemporary psychoanalysis has clearly moved a long way from the reductionism of Freud's unconscious drives. Even object relations theory is currently yielding to notions of inter-subjective fields. In much the same way as Newton was not negated by, but encompassed in, Einstein's larger four-dimensional perspective, these earlier psychoanalytic theories are not nullified by, but encompassed in, what must be seen as a multi-dimensional conceptual spectrum.

Can we usefully work in the fourth dimension? I suggest that many analysts already do, but prefer not to make it public for fear of exposing themselves as unorthodox. I do not doubt that they engage with their patients in "moments of meeting", but do not dignify them with a special name. If I call such moments "four-dimensional", it is to identify transformation as a specific but paradoxical, trans-rational, mutative process. Nor am I advocating radical departures from recognized good practice. As therapists we will carry on as before: listening to our clients with empathy, clarifying, challenging, and interpreting wherever seems appropriate. But perhaps we need to adopt a more modest attitude. We may know more psychology than our patients, but they know things we do not. Christianne, for example, had known far more childhood suffering than I ever did. She was also much more open to the numinous, but I could only recognize it when it was too late.

None of this is really new. Early in the last century Georg Groddeck wrote of a patient:

It was no longer important to give him instructions, to prescribe for him what might be right, but to change in such a way that he could use me. [Groddeck, 1923]

This recalls Winnicott's later approach, developed in his paper: "The use of an object", whereby the analyst repeatedly allows the patient to "destroy" him in order to find that he survives.

> From now on the subject says: "Hullo object!" "I destroyed you." "I love you." "You have value for me because of your survival of my destruction of you." "While I am loving you I am all the time destroying you in (unconscious) fantasy." [Winnicott, 1971]

Bollas speaks of the analyst becoming "situationally ill", and says:

> I am receptive to varying degrees of "madness" in myself occasioned by life in the patient's environment. In another area of myself, however, I am constantly there as an analyst: observing, assessing and holding that part of me that is necessarily ill. . . . In moments such as these who is the patient? . . . Indeed, in order to facilitate the analysand's cure, the analyst will often have occasion to treat his own illness first. [Bollas, 1987]

Bollas implies that, in healing himself, he heals the patient. I suggest that, in the same process, the patient heals him. I am proposing that it is not we who do the healing but, for want of a better name, the inter-subjective field brought into being by the patient–therapist relationship. By this means we give access to some ever-present, mysterious agency that uses us as its instrument. We might compare the therapist's function to that of a magnifying glass which, as most children discover, is capable of focusing the sun's rays to the point of setting paper alight. We can assist the healing power—whatever its source—by focusing our empathy, intelligence, skill, training, and experience to ensure that the maximum of light can pass through us. If, through our narcissism, we get in its way, the patient's soul will merely smoulder but not catch fire. Our capacity to help the patient consists, paradoxically, in giving up our omnipotent wish to cure, so that we may reach the point where we accept each patient just as they are, in the knowledge that acceptance is the only place from which change can begin.

CHAPTER TWO

Love, the aesthetic conflict and the self

Patricia Allen

In 1988 Dr Donald Meltzer and Meg Harris Williams wrote a book on "the role of the aesthetic conflict in development, art and violence". *The Apprehension of Beauty* added a new dimension to psychoanalytic thinking on development at that time. It was a dimension which suggested that Meltzer's thinking was close to the work of another great innovator, Dr Michael Fordham. While Meltzer's ideas grew from within the Kleinian tradition, Fordham was a follower of Jung. Fordham's work as a child psychiatrist and, later, analyst, led him to postulate a theory of early development. His model was based on Jung's concept of the self as the totality of the psyche with its personal and collective aspects and he demonstrated its relevance to infancy. Thus, Fordham brought to analytical psychology a coherent model of development. Whereas Jung's idea was of a self becoming active in mid-life through the process of individuation, Fordham's theory was that there exists a primary self, a primary state of integration, a psychosomatic unity, which deintegrates and reintegrates as the infant instigates a relationship with his mother. In *The Apprehension of Beauty*, the authors write imaginatively of the mental life of the foetus and the new-born. They say:

We cannot take the newborn child as a *tabula rasa* but must consider the possibility that emotional experiences, their symbolic representation in dream thought, and their impact on the structuring of the personality may commence in utero. [Meltzer & Harris Williams, 1988, p. 8]

The experience postulated here is one in which the infant is "dazzled" by his earliest encounters with the outside of his mother's body, her breasts, her eyes, her beauty. The passionate language conveys an experience that is vivid, full of emotion and conflict for the infant. At the centre of this conflict, it seems, is uncertainty, not knowing. The infant is overwhelmed by the impact of an object desired but enigmatic, and then he recoils. This new dimension in psychoanalytic thinking on development, represented by the aesthetic conflict, was based on extensive clinical experience over many years across the range of psychopathology:

The psychopathology, which we study and allege to treat, has its primary basis in the flight from pain of the aesthetic conflict. The impact of separation, of deprivation—emotional and physical, of physical illness, of oedipal conflict—pregenital and genital, of chance events, of seductions and brutality, of indulgence and over-protection, of family disintegration, of the death of parents or siblings—all of these derive the core of their significance for the developmental process from their contribution as aspects of the underlying, fundamental process of the avoidance of the impact of the beauty of the world and of passionate intimacy with another human being. [Meltzer & Harris Williams, 1988, p. 29]

Not having Meltzer's experience and brilliantly imaginative senses, most psychotherapists could only wonder and watch and listen with a new question in mind: is all psychopathology based on this recoil from the overwhelming experience of the beauty of the world, the mother, and the intimacy of her presence? The more I review my own clinical experience in the light of Meltzer's thinking on the aesthetic conflict, the more helpful I find the idea.

In this paper I would like to keep in mind the idea of psychoanalytical psychotherapy as enabling an individual to *return to* the state of a loving passionate involvement with a world from which he has much earlier fled in apprehension. I think that it is important to note that while Meltzer admits that there may be many babies who do not have beautiful mothers who find them beautiful babies, his experience convinces him otherwise. He writes: "There is much evidence (c.f. Spitz) to suggest that being thus untouched is not compatible with survival, or at least with survival of the mind" (Meltzer & Harris Williams, 1988, p. 29). I believe that this means we may think about emotional events in the consulting room in a way that takes account of the existence of an initial whole-ness, an initial or primary capacity for love, intimacy, and passion which has been wounded by overwhelming depressive anxiety. Of passion, Meltzer writes:

> The most adequate description . . . would seem to be that our emotions are engaged in such a way that love, hate and the yearn-ing for understanding are all set in motion. It is the consortium that is essential. [Meltzer & Harris Williams, 1988, p. 143]

In his review of *The Apprehension of Beauty* Michael Fordham wrote:

> To find the self in Jung's sense being rediscovered by a Kleinian is not altogether unexpected and it is gratifying, for in 1950 I suggested that Klein's model was congested and required a concept of the self. Jung used to remark that if what he discovered was passed over, somebody else would discover it. He did not add, as he might have done, in a different way, and even using a different language, but that is what I hold is happening. [Fordham, 1989, p. 300]

I believe it is legitimate for us to think of Fordham's concept of the "primary self" or "primary integrate" as close to and indeed converging with Meltzer's view of the new-born infant. Later in the same review Fordham wrote:

> Meltzer's book is extremely moving and adds a dimension to Bion's model building in that the aesthetic object is given a primacy along with O; this is further confirmation that he is referring to the self. If further evidence be needed he has come to understand that the whole object and the depressive position precede the paranoid schizoid position, a conclusion I had arrived at by a different route when considering the development of mental life in the infant. [Fordham, 1989, p. 300]

It is this idea of the aesthetic experience and the aesthetic conflict as qualities of the self which can, I believe, make a difference to the way in which we as psychotherapists think about our patients.

I understand that what Fordham thought to be "congested" in Klein's theory was her concept of the existence of a rudimentary ego from the beginning of life. He suggested that there exists a primary self or primary integrate which deintegrates and reintegrates as the infant begins to relate to his environment. Astor writes:

> In Fordham's work there is an original or primal self which is his way of describing the original integrate, the psychosomatic unity of the infant. This primary integrate is a phenomenonless state which develops by a process of deintegration and reintegration, with each reintegration forming a new dynamic equilibrium within the infant. The self as Fordham described it was the instigator as much as the receptor of infant experience. [Astor, 1995, p. 237]

In the more ordinary, everyday language of infant observation, we see a sleeping infant stir, making little movements with his body, particularly perhaps with his mouth and tongue, as he wakes and cries. If his mother responds thoughtfully and understands that her baby is hungry she will talk to him, possibly telling him that she knows he is hungry, and she will feed him. He will eventually fall asleep again digesting not simply milk but the emotional experience of being fed.

Applying Fordham's theory to this sequence we may say that in response to hunger the infant begins a process of deintegration or unpacking of the psychosomatic unity of the self. His archetypal or innate predisposition to find a breast and nipple is met by the actual breast offered to him by his mother, and if all goes well he will reintegrate this experience. Repeated deintegrative and reintegrative experiences will develop the infant's awareness of his mother and his environment. From this I think we can see that Fordham believed that ego is developed out of the deintegrative and reintegrative processes of the self.

Fordham arrived at the concept of a primary self through analytical work with children and over many years developed a model which he could apply to research into infant observation. Astor explains further:

Fordham's language keeps pathology and development separate. He perceives the deintegrate's continuity with the wholeness of the self as serving the emotional development of the individual, without splitting being necessary, unless something goes wrong. He is also reluctant to attribute to the infant ego what he feels is better described as a quality of the self. [Astor, 1995, p. 63]

In 1986 the *Journal of Analytical Psychology* devoted an issue to the work of Fordham, its founder. "Michael Fordham reviewed" contained a tribute from Donald Meltzer. It also contained Proner's paper entitled "Defences of the self and envy of oneself", after Fordham's 1974 paper "Defences of the self". In his paper Proner writes of an anorexic new-born who appeared not to be persecuted by the prospect of a bad experience but to object to receiving the goodness of the breast. He compares Meltzer's ideas on the apprehension of beauty to Jungian thought:

There is profound pain in the initial "apprehension" of what might in Jungian thought correspond to the *numinous*. I have found in many patients that beauty, linked with goodness, can be almost too much to bear. This can be nothing to do with envy nor with persecutory feelings in general but with something which can only be described, if at all, in poetry. [Proner, 1986, p. 277 (my italics)]

Here in Proner's paper we begin to see how the aesthetic experience can be a cause of depressive pain.

This reference to the numinous, perhaps a concept some of us are reluctant to use because of the ease with which it can be traduced, is, I believe, used properly here. Jung described it thus:

The numinosum is a dynamic agency or effect not caused by an arbitrary act of will. On the contrary, it seizes and controls the human subject, who is always its victim rather than its creator.

The numinosum is either a quality belonging to a visible object or the influence of an invisible presence that causes a peculiar alteration of consciousness. [Jung, C.W. 11, para. 6]

I think that the alteration of consciousness which accompanies an encounter with a loved and therefore beautiful person or with a work of painting, music, or poetry, which moves us deeply, which is almost too much to bear, is both rare and familiar. It is not an ordinary or everyday state of mind and is usually beyond the power of most of us to put into words. I suspect my hesitation over the word *numinous* to be both a fear of traducing something precious, which should perhaps remain nameless, and also perhaps a fear of the thought itself: that there can and does exist such an experience which is so precious we hardly dare inhabit it. Of course, we might, if our senses are so disturbed. We might respond out of a feeling of hate, wishing to destroy what disturbs us, but in Meltzer's view this would be secondary to our feeling of awe and wonder. In a recent paper Adams writes of the profound impact on some patients when they discover, through analytic work with their dreams, that they possess a rich inner world. She does not use the word "self" to describe this world but she does liken the profound impact of its discovery to the child's reaction to the beauty of the object, as described by Meltzer. "There is a sense of enigma and separateness about the dream which makes it impossible to control and possess as is the mother for the child" (Adams, 2002, p. 21).

I am reminded of a patient who greeted me by looking at me oh, so briefly and then dropping her eyes. When we were able to talk about these fleeting moments she said: "I can't bear to see the warmth in your eyes; I can't bear to think that you might be pleased to see me." She conveyed to me her anxiety lest she should take for granted something which felt so precious and so precarious. There occurred a similar happening with another patient, a young man in his twenties who was able to unpack many of his feelings over time. He had begun his therapy by looking straight into my eyes and smiling sweetly. I did not find the experience sweet, I felt controlled. I felt that he wished to enter my mind and take over my emotional response. I felt that he was trying to compel me to find him a sweet and charming person.

As the therapy progressed he sometimes found it difficult to look at me at all. I understood this as his envy and resentment, his wish not to see me as a separate individual who could see him in a way which he did not ordain. More recently he said: "When I saw you today you looked somehow filled with light—I realized what I had been missing by not looking at you. Then I immediately had another thought: Do I smell? Would I put you off?" My sense was of my patient having a fleeting encounter with his aesthetic object in the transference relationship. His second thought, that I might find him smelly and be put off by him was, I believe, a manifestation of anxiety of a depressive nature. He could find me beautiful but I would be repulsed by him. I believe that he had contacted in himself a sense of being small, insignificant, and bad in relation to his object and that this was compounded by his phantasies of intrusion and control. The moment was lost; the shining light was darkened by anxiety. The moment at which I could find him not *sweet* but honest, open, and loving was lost. I think that *what* was lost to us in that moment was what Meltzer has characterized as "aesthetic reciprocity".

In a recent book which celebrates the work of Donald Meltzer, Gianna Williams has written a chapter entitled "Reflections on 'aesthetic reciprocity'". Williams describes a baby and mother:

> ... who were both capable of sustaining the pain of experiencing one another as precious. The baby, aged two months, would move away from the breast after the first few hungry sucks and look up into mother's eyes (this happened repeatedly), giving her a white smile as his mouth was full of milk. The gratitude and reciprocal appreciation that came across in that observation, when the baby was still so tiny, gives support to one of the very important statements made by Meltzer in connection with the aesthetic conflict ... He suggests that depressive feelings and the experience of an object as infinitely precious and beautiful are *primary*. [Williams, 2000, pp. 138–139]

This lovely vignette does, as Williams says, suggest aesthetic reciprocity, mother and baby finding each other precious and beautiful. It also suggests to me what Fordham understood as the continuity of the deintegrative experience, in this case feeding and being fed, with the self. Neither is split; we might say that the whole of the baby grasps the whole of the mother that he perceives. It is wholehearted!

When we encounter such moments in the consulting room it is often after much struggle and pain. Williams suggests that such patients who have to *recapture* the perception of their object as beautiful in the transference are subject to powerful phantasies of controlling it, possessing it, and robbing it of its essence (Williams, 2000, pp. 143–144). I have noticed that in some patients' material there appears a beautiful loved child, sometimes an adult with child-like qualities, for whom the patient *becomes* the therapist mother. The love and understanding which is lavished on this child, who is never allowed to experience need, feel small, or be humiliated, is a lesson to the therapist. It is also a way of feeding vicariously by feeding and never being fed. It is a recognizable narcissistic mechanism of defence which takes over the qualities of the therapist and projectively identifies the needy child in another. The therapist is then left to experience admiration and awe at this "mock-up" of aesthetic reciprocity.

One patient, a single woman who was childless, reported a dream in which she had a child. She lifted the child into her arms and experienced a blissful feeling, knowing what it was like to be the centre of the child's world, the mummy person. I refer to these situations as "mock-ups" because they have the quality of mocking the therapist, making her feel useless in comparison with the patient, and because they convey the idea of a modelling for the purpose of a rehearsal.

In contrast, in other patients there appears to be a more perverse and destructive aim, to destroy love and anything that could be conceived of as beautiful. Far from being a precious and mutually satisfying experience, feeding can mean only a process where poison is ingested, often in an addictive way. A patient who was addicted to chocolate would say to me, as he grew larger and larger, "Psychotherapy is crap but it's all I can ever have." He was tragically stuck in a world of his own poisonous projections.

Patients like these can declare bloody war on the therapist and on the idea that there can be a loving situation which can be emotionally nourishing. These are patients who identify with the dead and dying. Another patient, whose recourse was to alcohol rather than analysis, talked of "the rotting carcass that is my inner self". He controlled the therapist by, as he described it, "putting the batteries in when I'm with you and taking them out when I leave". His need for control was such that he turned me into a mechanical mother and his own mind into a machine. His life was dedicated to efficiency and professional success. In rare moments he could admit that, although musical, he could not go to a concert for fear of being overwhelmed by feeling. I believe that the same rigid control with which he refused the aesthetic experience was necessary in relation to the loving and emotional mother in the transference. The nature of the transference relationship, with its overtones of dominance and control, suggested not simply hate but the fear of loss if something as precious as love were allowed to be.

Another patient, a woman in her forties, was subject to particular experiences of domination and persecution each time she told me anything of her vulnerable feelings and her need for love. A powerful internal voice would mock her with the words: "Why did you tell her that?" Whenever therapy threatened to put her in touch with feelings of love and her need for intimacy she was threatened from within. After one session in which she had, I believe, felt touched by love she brought a dream. She was trapped, a prisoner in her room. Outside her window motorbikers clad in black leather patrolled up and down in the darkness. This seemed a graphic description of her internal situation where the loving and vulnerable part of her personality was held in a state of siege by darker elements. These men of darkness made certain that her connection with her therapist was broken and she was trapped in her isolation. I have noticed that in the material of some patients such "gang" dreams or associations come together with images of darkness. The "gang" formation written about by Meltzer (1967), Rosenfeld (1971), and Williams (1997) is a powerful and destructive internal organization which appears to offer protection against the pain and suffering inherent in loving and being dependent upon another person. Williams made an interesting distinction when she wrote: "Gangs offer to their members something which groups do not, protection against pain." Rather like the Mafia and its protection racket, if the individual adheres to the system, pays his dues, obeys the rules, one of which is inevitably secrecy, he or she is protected. The gang with its associations of adolescence and delinquency is anti-parental, anti-family, and ultimately sterile. It promises protection while it subjugates the individual to the darkness of its own distorted relationship with truth, with thinking as an individual, and with love. This domination by the forces of darkness in the personality seems to me to suggest what may have been an earlier darkening of the light when a rigid splitting was the only recourse in the face of what I suspect was a cruel experience of the aesthetic

conflict. The patient quoted above said: "My mother was so beautiful—I would have killed for one of her smiles!'

In trying to understand my patient's impulse to kill for one of
her beautiful mother's smiles it seems necessary to understand that
the mind that kills is not really the mind that apprehends her
beauty, but it pretends to be. This was borne out within the transference relationship when her attempts to make me smile resulted
in an impasse because my response was one of fearing for my life,
my analytic life at least. I felt controlled and robbed of my auton-
omy. My patient's gradual realization of her controlling and
murderous phantasies towards me gave rise to intense anxieties lest
she should lose me. Over time, as a more truthful relationship
became possible between us, her feelings of loss, regret, and mourning became more available. She expressed much sadness that she
hadn't known earlier in life what she knew now. I believe that it is
the most poignant part of any therapy when a patient appears to be
able to value knowing and understanding through experience but
is then faced with the knowledge of opportunities lost and feelings
of regret. Sadness, regret, and also a feeling that they should have
known characterize these times. Is this a feeling that relates to the
idea of a primary aesthetic object and an original aesthetic conflict?
I think it is likely that it has to do with what Bion (1962) called the
K-link.

In Meltzer's terms the yearning for understanding is, with love
and hate, the consortium that is necessary for passionate involvement. It is, I understand, at the centre of the aesthetic conflict as
he describes it. Both this yearning and the K-link are, I believe,
further developments of the idea formulated by Freud and taken
up and developed by Klein, epistemophilia. Recently, Britton has
suggested that we think of epistemophilic development as complicated by, and merged with, love and hate but not deriving from
them.

> I think it is better to say that we love things, hate things and want to
> know things rather than speak of abstract drives. [Britton, 1998, p. 3]

So what of patients who cannot bear to know their object?
Perhaps it is possible to imagine that somewhere, at some time,
maybe very long ago, in almost another world, they have known

the goodness and beauty of their object and fled from its impact. We abandon the consortium of love, hate, and the yearning for understanding, and resort to splitting because the aesthetic experience is hard to bear. In doing so we weaken a function of our own minds. Meltzer wrote:

> ... in the interplay of joy and pain, engendering the love (L) and hate (H) links of ambivalence, it is the quest for understanding (K-link) that rescues the relationship from impasse. [Meltzer & Harris Williams, 1988, p. 28]

Earlier I suggested that treating aesthetic experience and the aesthetic conflict as primary, as having a great deal in common with Fordham's understanding of the self, may be a valuable addition to the ways in which we think about our patients. I think that to understand the pain of the aesthetic experience is to understand how it could be a source of torment to be forever "seized by the *numinosum*". For the therapist, I think that to be able to bear hatred, rage, envy, being possessed, invaded, made to feel one's work is useless, futile, having one's words divested of meaning, are all more bearable if we can understand these as ways of avoiding the pain of the impact of intimacy and passion—ambivalence. We cannot think of love without hate and now we cannot think of love and hate without thinking about understanding. The link of knowledge that Bion is emphasizing with the links of love and hate refers to an emotional experience. It is an emotional experience that is characterized by pain or frustration, the frustration of having to learn from experience (Bion, 1962).

From Bion's work we understand that an emotional experience cannot be conceived of in isolation from a relationship. The link is between a subject which tries to know an object and an object which can be known (Grinberg *et al.*, 1975). For an infant it is the availability of his mother's mind as a container that he needs in order to develop. The mother's mind, and particularly her capacity for reverie, are essential for the transformation of primitive experiences that would otherwise leave him in a world full of his own projected intolerable feelings. My patient who was addicted to chocolate felt that in psychotherapy he was doomed to be fed his own crap. There was nothing else. He appeared to have no sense of an object that could mediate or detoxify his projections. This was a patient who was sure he could never be loved. Again, in *Learning From Experience*, Bion writes of the mother's capacity to relate to her infant: "Leaving aside the physical channels of communication my impression is that her love is expressed by reverie" (Bion, 1962). What we, as psychotherapists, seek to manifest for our patients is just that quality of being that is concerned with getting to know, getting to understand, learning from experience.

It would seem to be the pain and fear of the unknown fate of what is a precious experience that drives us towards dividing our world and ourselves. When we allow emotional experience to take hold of us without this division then we retain our connection and our continuity with the self, our potential for wholeness, our consortium. We might say after Meltzer that the aesthetic conflict and depressive anxiety are primary. This is in line with Fordham's concept of the self as a primary integrate with its deintegrates capable of retaining the self's potential for wholeness. If we want to find love then we can only find it along with the other members of the consortium. As Britton puts it:

> We want to love, to hate and to know our objects, and we also need to be loved, fear being hated and want to be understood. Internally we are inclined to love ourselves, loathe ourselves and want to understand ourselves. [Britton, 1998, p. 3]

CHAPTER THREE

The emerging religious dimension of knowing in psychoanalysis

Steven Mendoza

Introduction

Freud treated religion as an illusory belief system explaining natural phenomena and establishing inhibitors of instinctual drives as a pseudo-moral system-regulating behaviour. Religious experience, as against religious belief and religious observance, he seems to have dismissed as an oceanic, that is manic, process even more divorced than belief from the function of the ego to test reality. Bion, an impeccable scholar of Freud, writes in 1967 as though he expects us to take for granted "experience of God", "religious awe", "ineffable experience". He says, "The psychoanalyst accepts the reality of reverence and awe." Commenting in 1967 on his earlier paper "Notes on the theory of schizophrenia", on the complementary senses of memory and desire, he explains:

> ... There needs to be a recognized formulation which is understood by all psycho-analysts to display the invariants in an event which is unconscious because obscured by memory, *although* it has happened, and an event which is manifest because disclosed by desire though it has *not* happened. Memory and desire may be regarded as past and future "senses" (analogous to the mathematical concept of "sense" and applying indifferently to time or

space) of the same "thing". Making use of sense in this way a formulation "*desire*" would have the same value as "*memory*", the former referring to an event that had happened and the latter referring to an event that had not happened and therefore not usually described as being "remembered". A patient who could be described in terms of conversational English as "remembering" something that had *not* happened would resemble a patient who was described as hallucinated. Conversely the patient who did *not* remember what *had* happened, through the operation of "*desire*", or *remembered* what had *not* happened, through the operation of the same agency, should likewise be recognized as belonging to the same underlying group of "hallucinosis".

The concept of "sense" which I have introduced has not been recognized in psycho-analytical practice and the psycho-analyst's armoury has been correspondingly deficient in observations of omnipotence and omniscience. [Bion, 1967, pp 143–144]

The Concise Oxford English Dictionary (1990, p. 1102) gives as the ninth out of nine meanings of the word "sense" this mathematical definition:

9   Math. etc. **a** a direction of movement. **b** that which distinguishes a pair of entities which differ only in that each is the reverse of the other.

If we break up this passage into a series of discrete statements it is easier to see the equivalencies and disparities Bion is proposing:

"Memory and desire may be regarded as past and future 'senses' ... of the same 'thing'".

Making use of sense in this way a formulation "*desire*" would have the same value as "*memory*",
the former referring to an event that had happened
and the latter referring to an event that had not happened
and therefore not usually described as being "remembered".

A patient who could be described in terms of conversational English as "remembering" something that had *not* happened would resemble a patient who was described as hallucinated.

Conversely the patient who did *not* remember what *had* happened, through the operation of "*desire*",

or *remembered* what had *not* happened,
through the operation of the same agency, (*"desire"*),

should likewise be recognized as belonging to the same underlying group of "hallucinosis".

It appears that when *"desire"* looks back at what *did* happen, it
is equivalent to memory. A colleague, Patricia Allen, suggests that
this may be like fantasy recalling the realization of desire. And
when it looks back at what did *not* happen, it is hallucinatory.

It seems that *"memory"* "remembers" what has *not* happened
and is also hallucinatory.

So it seems that although in absolute terms *"memory"* and
"desire" are merely senses of the same function, *"memory"* is always
hallucinatory but *"desire"* *may* "remember" what really did happen.
As always in Bion's writing, greater efforts to analyse his syntax
and to find in his formulations realizations from the reader's experience help us to think his thoughts.

A correct understanding of the intent of this passage may be that
although *"memory"* and *"desire"* are merely senses of the same
function they are both false consciousness which saturates an experience with sensual (C category elements) preventing a religious
experience being known as such and allowing only an experience
which is transferential.

* * *

Having explained how memory and desire may be different senses
of the same thing Bion goes on to show how this idea may enable
an analyst to distinguish a distorted view of the father from an
incapacity for direct experience of God:

> ... It is quite common for psycho-analytic students to observe
> patients whose references to God betray the operation of "memo-
> ries" of the father. The term "God" is seen to indicate the scale by
> which the magnitude, wisdom and strength of the father is to be
> measured. If the psycho-analyst preserved an open mind to the
> mental phenomena unfolding in the psycho-analytical experience
> he would be free to appreciate the significance of sense as I have
> described it above. As a consequence he would not be restricted to

interpretations of God as displaying a distorted view of the father, but would be able to assess evidence, should it present itself, for supposing that the analysand was incapable of direct experience of God and that experience of God had not occurred, because it was made impossible by the existence of "$\overrightarrow{desires}$" and "$\overrightarrow{memories}$".

The experiences sketched out in 39[1] indicate the degree to which "$\overrightarrow{memory}$" and "$\overleftarrow{desire}$" obstruct the patient's relationship to an absent breast or penis on a level of mind, or at a time of life, when such an object would be so important as to evoke feelings analogous to what would in an adult be religious awe. This could be represented by desire. Taking the evidence in its other aspect, the sense memory, its significance would be its disclosure to the extent to which the patient's relationship with God was disturbed by sensuously desired models (or C category elements) which prevented an ineffable experience by their concreteness and therefore unsuitability to represent the realization. In religious terms, this experience would seem to be represented by statements that the erring race or individual allowed itself to be beguiled by graven images, idols, religious statuary, or, in psycho-analysis, the idealized analyst. Interpretations should be given, based on the recognition of desire, but not that they should be derived and given from recognition of the sense memory. The need for such appreciation and interpretation is far reaching. It would extend psycho-analytic theory to cover the views of mystics from the Bhagavad Gita to the present. The psycho-analyst accepts the reality of reverence and awe, the possibility of a disturbance in the individual which makes atonement[2] and, therefore, an expression of reverence and awe impossible. The central postulate is that atonement with ultimate reality, or O, as I have called it to avoid involvement with an existing association, is essential to harmonious mental growth. It follows that interpretation involves elucidation of evidence touching atonement, and not evidence only of the continuing operation of immature relationship with a father. The introduction of "sense" or "direction" involves extensions of existing psycho-analytical theory. Disturbance in capacity for atonement is associated with megalomanic attitudes. [Bion, 1967a, p. 144]

Bion wrote (1967b, p. 17) of "the psychoanalyst's intuition of the reality with which he must be at one". I think Bion writes above of atonement as at-one-ment, intending to link the integration of the depressive position with the capacity to have an experience of God instead of having to resort to the sight and sound and smell of an idealized father.

> Taking the evidence in its other aspect, the sense memory, its significance would be its disclosure to the extent to which the patient's relationship with God was disturbed by sensuously desired models (or C category elements) which prevented an ineffable experience by their concreteness and therefore unsuitability to represent the realization. In religious terms, this experience would seem to be represented by statements that the erring race or individual allowed itself to be beguiled by graven images, idols, religious statuary, or, in psycho-analysis, the idealized analyst. [Bion, 1967a, p. 145]

In repeating this quotation I am emphasizing how Bion brings to psychoanalysis the religious principle of renouncing the sensual world so as to leave room for religious experience. This is often understood as an ascetic practice of renunciation on moral grounds. In the quest for knowledge of God by the religious it is undertaken not as a moral repudiation of sin but as a practice instrumental to success. The principle of abstinence in psychoanalytic practice seems to be a direct equivalent. Certainly its purpose is instrumental and not moral. In Buddhism renunciation is regarded not as the renunciation of pleasure but of suffering, since our craving for sensual pleasure and our clinging to what we believe will sustain us ultimately causes suffering rather than the pleasure and security it seeks.

Where he writes of "sensuously desired models (or C category elements) which prevent an ineffable experience by their concreteness", this idea may be explained by Meltzer's (1988) idea of aesthetic conflict where the apprehension of beauty (the ineffable) may overwhelm the psyche so that it resorts to splitting, forsaking the depressive position because it is unbearable.

It seems that when Bion wrote psychoanalytically of religion his religious ideas were correct. It is customary to think of his religious knowledge as derived from his childhood sojourn in the east. It may be that actually his knowledge was, in the terms that will be explored, an evolution of the "O" of religion into his psychoanalytic conceptions. To find contents for his notoriously unsaturated formulations requires an understanding of the psychoanalytic meanings of religion, or rather, religious experience.

He wrote: "The central postulate is that atonement[2] with ultimate reality, or O, as I have called it to avoid involvement with an
existing association, is essential to harmonious mental growth."
This postulate may be taken as a principle of psychic development
depending upon "atonement with ultimate reality". But it may
mean more. It may mean that religious experience confers a
"harmonious mental growth" which constitutes the development of
an organization which confers advantages of cognitive capacity to
construct reality and emotional quality of life. It has always been
held in religion that religion makes a person a better person and
that personal development is incomplete without religious experience. Perhaps the valid conclusion is that "atonement with ultimate
reality" is *both* a psychological being at one with and a religious
one, that there is not always a difference between the two.

With the idea of "O" and its evolutions into consciousness goes
Bion's injunction to abjure memory and desire. This helps us to
understand why religion has always held that the senses, and the
saturation of experience that they impose, stand in the way of religious as well as analytic experience. This is very different from the
moral proscriptions ascribed to religion by Freud.

* * *

A section from Lao Tzu is remarkable for being on the one hand a
religious text of Taoism and on the other hand full of connotations
which are evocatively psychoanalytic.

48   The multitude are joyous
      As if partaking of the *t'ai lao* offering
      Or going up to a terrace in spring.
      I alone am inactive and reveal no signs,
      And wax without having reached the limit.
      Like a baby that has not learned to smile,
      Listless as though with no home to go back to.
      The multitude all have more than enough.
      I alone seem to be in want.
      My mind is like that of a fool – how blank!
      Vulgar people are clear.
      I alone am drowsy.
      Vulgar people are alert.
      I alone am muddled.

> Calm like the sea;
> Like a high wind that never ceases
> The multitude all have a purpose.
> I alone am foolish and uncouth.
> I alone am different from others
> And value being fed by the mother.
>
> [Lao Tzu, 1963, p. 24]

The poem seems to anticipate psychoanalysis in its tolerance of infantile dependency as the condition of psychic integrity. There is a note of narcissistic schizoid aloofness to be heard in the piece. But it can also be heard as sincere in its profession that although the worldly are knowing there is a knowledge that only innocence allows. This sense of knowing something very simple but also fundamental may be useful to the consideration of ideas which might otherwise seem complicated and which are, after all, esoteric. But so is psychoanalysis, because knowable only through experience, esoteric.

Contrition, penitence, redemption, grace

The fundamental religious experience must be the original animist panic which feels something greater than the self both without, immanent in nature, and within. With this sense of the divine goes a realization that goodness is inherently pleasurable and obviously right. If we do not know these phenomena by experience we know them by report. They are psychological objects, states of mind, emotional experiences: "The psycho-analyst accepts the reality of reverence and awe" (Bion, 1967a, p. 144). Such phenomena are explained by different disciplines in their own terms. Thus metapsychology, and particularly the psychoanalytic school of Melanie Klein, writes of the depressive position. As is well known, this term uses the name of a psychiatric illness to label a normal, indeed benign, organization. It is named thus because it is when we acknowledge the anger and resentment we feel towards what we most love that, apprehending its wholeness, we enter a world of whole objects; a world of mourning for lost objects, murdered in phantasy, but also a world of beauty, a real world in which we seek to make reparation for the damage we realize we have done.

The process of confession and redemption is much closer to the analysis of the depressive position than is indicated by the reputation of the Catholic church for persecution and retribution. The psychoanalytical process of acknowledging the guilt for an inner object enviously attacked, and the process of mourning its loss, continue as reparation for that loss and the finding again of a good object. In the depressive position guilt is possible, instead of persecutory apprehension. In Catholicism forgiveness follows contrition. Sometimes the persecutory, retaliatory, sadistic impulses of the paranoid organization persist. Sometimes the church projects these outside itself, as when heretics were handed over to the secular arm to suffer cruel treatment and even death, torture, burning at the stake.

The depressive position as atonement has a lot in common with the Jewish Day of Atonement: Time is taken to look at what was thought and said and done, or what it was wished to do. This kind of regret allows a state of integrity, no longer divided by denial. To speak of a good relationship with God or a good relationship with the self may refer to much the same state of mind: one that does not feel alone, that has wisdom, that rejoices in the aesthetic, created and meaningful.

In a 1998 concert programme note, the composer Takemitsu wrote: ". . . the joy of music ultimately seems connected with sadness, the sadness is that of existence.". The essence of the depressive position is that we can bear to find a good object inside us, that object being the mother or, in a more infantile state, the breast. But to call it mother or breast is a metapsychological imputation of the experience. The experience is actual and may be of something both inside and outside. It may not be the self but, for an adult, it is not usually Mummy either. Similarly religion may impute this same experience as an awareness of God. But we do not know God in the form prescribed by the dogma or iconography of religion. This immaculate nature of experience, uncontaminated by attribution and imputation, is the sense of knowing now emerging in psychoanalysis, particularly in the work of Bion and Meltzer, and also in Segal's (1991) understanding of aesthetics.

Many think that Martin Buber held the view that "God is not a person". But we understand that we apprehend Him by projecting the quality of a person onto Him.

Who is the third who walks always beside you?
When I count there are only you and I together   360
But when I look ahead up the white road
There is always another one walking beside you
Gliding wrapt in a brown mantle, hooded
I know not whether a man or a woman
—But who is that on the other side of you?

[Eliot, 1922, p. 65]

The essence of religion may be the actual experience, the appre-hension of "something"; psychoanalysis may call it an "object". Whether the experience is called psychological or theological is secondary to the actuality of the experience. Thus Meltzer:

> ... It remained for Melanie Klein, in her greatest formulation, the paranoid–schizoid and depressive positions to discover the economic principles regulating the relation of Ego to the Super-ego-(ideal) as the foundation of value. This material, as I have said, illustrates the metamorphosis of the super-ego-ideal, through the abandoning of defences, splitting processes in particular. The acceptance of integration and the assimilation into the super-ego-ideal by introjection also makes clear the paradox, so contrary to common sense, that *the most evolved part of an individual's mind lies beyond the experience of self and is apprehended as object*. The problem which every theological and philosophical system has attempted to grapple has finally found its proper venue, psychic reality. A new proof of the existence of God has evolved most unexpectedly through an essentially iconoclastic method which has at the same time fused this concept of God with that of individual mind, thus putting an end for all time to the possibility of religion as a social institution beyond the participation of the individual. God is dead in the outside world and brought to life within, but only, as we know, through mourning. It would be a good historical joke if it were to turn out that a Jew had carried the reformation to its logical end-point. [Meltzer, 1973, p. 78 (my italics)]

In making the point that *"the most evolved part of an individual's mind lies beyond the experience of self and is apprehended as object"* I think Meltzer means that the self is sensed as impersonal. Jung too treats of the self as having an impersonal quality of simply being—aloof above the sense of me and mine. The verb "to be" can take no object; we can only be what are. It is because of our insecurity that we try to assume an identity. This is where Bion (1962b, Ch.16) differentiates *learning from experience* from *knowing as the possession of objects of knowledge*. The more we try to *be* something, the less we *are* it. More and more this leads me to think of narcissism as the primary pathology: Paradoxically it seems that to accept that our nature is divine is *less* grandiose than to strive for power and status.

In tantric Buddhism this is called the adoption of pure view: To identify as a deity manifesting the Buddha Nature, the Buddha-hood latent in every sentient being, is closer to our real nature. It has the special negative validity of *not* identifying with perceived, attributed, qualities. To attribute to the self the qualities we usually think of as our own is held to be to impute upon the self a subjective impression, to adopt a deluded view. Deluded here means something very close to what in psychoanalysis would be called projective identification. The self is a percept, a mental object. We project into our inner world an image of the self and we identify with it. Those who feel themselves to be threatened with the lack of identity or threatened with the loss of it are those most likely to identify with such a projection. It is invalid to believe ourselves really to be the person that we seem to ourselves to be. The sense of a *real* self is merely the imputation of inherent existence to a phenomenon of self perception. When Meltzer says that *"the most evolved part of an individual's mind lies beyond the experience of self and is apprehended as object"*, this cultural precedent supports his contention and encourages us to try to grasp what he means.

When Jung writes of the self he means always the totality of our being, the conscious and the unconscious, the personal and the collective. In the writings of the post-Kleinians we also begin to read of the self but there the word is used ambiguously, sometimes of the ego and sometimes the whole of the self. In Hinduism the latter might be very close to Brahma. In Buddhism it is the Buddha Nature. In Judaism and the related religions, Christianity, Islam, there appears to be a greater separation between man and God. Perhaps the real difference is the gulf between human vanity and divinity. Psychoanalytically, to think of our sense of potential as divine means to impress upon ourselves the emotion of awe and the mindset of heightened awareness

Psychotherapy is very matter-of-fact in its aspirations. Freud said he could only restore people to ordinary human unhappiness.

The depressive position seems to me to be presented more and more as an ideal of organization to which we aspire in self-analysis. In the ideal of orientation to reality in the depressive position, proper feeling, psychoanalysis finds a sense of human potential that is religious.

When Meltzer (*ibid.*) writes of God being brought to life only through mourning, he must mean the association here between the depressive acknowledgement of the murdered object and the crucifixion. This myth of the king who must die is, after all, the theme of Frazer's *The Golden Bough* (1922), the book which took us back before the limited assimilation we had made of Classical learning to a deeper understanding of the wisdom that it is the purpose of myth to evoke. Winnicott (1971, p. 105) writes of the good always being destroyed and always surviving: *"'Hullo, object!' 'I destroyed you.' 'I love you.' 'You have value for me because of your survival of my destruction of you.'"* The capacity for concern which underlies this object relation is "... used to cover in a positive way a phenomenon that is covered in a negative way by the word 'guilt'". (1963, p. 73).

The internal parents

From the apprehension of the most evolved part of the mind not as an experience of self but as object, Meltzer goes on to describe the duality of the object itself as the internal parents. He writes of internal objects derived from the introjection of external parents. Winnicott's (1971) transitional object is important here for development because of its quality of having both internal and external manifestations. But this is a matter not merely of the internal object and the self, but of the internal couple. In "Attacks on linking", Bion (1959) advances the understanding of the Oedipus complex. Using the model of container/contained he shows how the link between the internal couple is the means of thinking. The intercourse of the internal couple conceives the children of the mind: ideas, knowledge, experience. "Conceptions" is a common metaphor for thoughts.

The paradox remains; that the best aspect of the mind is beyond self and the self must evolve in its relation to its internal objects through dependence, ripening to obedience, and ending as the acceptance of *inspired independence. Under their aegis!* If this theory is correct, the conclusion is inescapable that man is a fool to defend himself against the mental pains by which disharmony between self and super-ego-ideal is manifest. The spectrum of pains, the pains of the depressive position, herald discord and call for parley, the self-analytic process. The pains are the price we pay for having good objects and, considering their preciousness, they are comically inexpensive. But this should not surprise us since the generosity of the breast is the soul of the combined object.

While the paradox of the me and the not-me is intriguing, the beauty of the system is rather overpowering in its biology. Where natural selection operates externally, individual selection dominates the growth and change of the super-ego-ideal. As Freud stressed, the *figure* of the internal objects derives largely from the primitive introjection of the parents (modified of course by the contribution of projection and projective identification) during the period of maximal dependence on these external persons. But thereafter introjection of qualities proceeds under the sway of admiration. [Meltzer, 1973, p. 78]

According to Meltzer (*ibid.*, p. 79): ". . . introjection of qualities proceeds under the sway of admiration". Admiration requires humility. Humility can bear to attribute creativity to the internal parents. Narcissism would appropriate their acts to the self. That is why he writes:

the best aspect of the mind is beyond self and the self must evolve in its relation to its internal objects through dependence, ripening to obedience, and ending as the acceptance of *inspired independence. Under their aegis!* [Meltzer, *ibid.*, p. 78]

Meltzer speaks of inspiration under the aegis of the mind's own internal objects, the internal couple. The mother's capacity to understand her infant is the first manifestation of container/contained in development. Her mind digests projections of impulses that the infant's mind cannot stand. The nipple in the mouth and the penis in the vagina are models of container/contained. The thought is the contained, the mind the container. In Bion's (1962b) theory of thinking we come to an idea in the mind as the psychic realization of the model of container/contained. In Tantric Buddhism the parents in embrace are Deities but they are also called father and mother. In their form they may be depicted in the coitus of familiar oriental iconography. But in their nature they are held to be aspects of the Buddha. Post-Kleinian psychoanalysis has come to see that the capacity to retain, unmurdered, the internal couple as a good object is essential to the capacity to think. What had been seen in the west as oriental sensuality, or fornication, turns out to be the dissolution of the Oedipus complex.

When Meltzer writes of the evolution of the self through dependence on internal objects he does not refer to development sustained by the care of the external parents. He refers to psychic evolution through the ministry of internal objects. Their not-me quality takes the self beyond the egotistical consciousness of the narcissistic organization. He wrote: "... individual selection dominates the growth and change of the super-ego-ideal" (ibid., p. 78). His choice of the word "evolution" instead of the psychological word "development" suggests not so much the biological sense of evolution as the spiritual sense of the evolution of the individual to a psychic organization that transcends the personal. Transcendence is sometimes given a manic quality of ecstatic transports and divine visitation, as in Freud's discussion of the oceanic. It also implies transcendence of self, a sense of the existence of others, an objectivity of consciousness, a sense of being a custodian of a common consciousness. Many of us have known this occasionally as an emotional experience of joy and seriousness. Perhaps Freud, for all his creativity, was never vouchsafed a sense of the wonder of his own discovery or any understanding of the valid religious experience this comprises. For Jung, the Transcendent Function is the surmounting of the good and bad polarities of the archetypes to realize what Klein might call whole objects.

Psychoanalysis, like biology, teaches us that the need for not-self objects is unavoidable. In Buddhism, the psychic process of meeting this need is called "refuge". Refuge is refuge from fear, suffering or danger. The three objects of refuge are the Buddha, the Dharma, or teachings—literally truth, and the Sangha, spiritual community. Each of these has psychoanalytic equivalents but the principle of refuge itself is fundamental. Sometimes it is only through seeking refuge that we can find the cessation of suffering. Psychoanalytically, the point is always to relinquish the narcissistic, egocentric organization and to acknowledge the need for something greater than the self. At first psychoanalysis presented this as the need to stay in touch with a regressed part of us that depended in an infantile way on parents.

> As Freud stressed, the figure of the internal objects derives largely from the primitive introjection of the parents . . . during the period of maximal dependence on these external persons. But thereafter introjection of qualities proceeds under the sway of admiration. [Meltzer, *ibid.*, p. 79]

Under the sway of admiration we may introject qualities which are more adult. It is by introjecting them that we evolve. Thus the student of *Dharma* may realize the qualities of the refuge object by introjection. He may become a refuge object himself. He becomes so by virtue of his capacity to give refuge from suffering to others. He does this by his capacity to teach which includes being a realization of refuge himself. Refuge and introjection under the sway of admiration are similar. They share three things: first, the dependence on non-self objects; second, the dual nature these objects have of being both internal and external; and third, the way that, although the quality of dependency is emotional in an infantile way, its nature or function is the development of adult faculties through introjection. Introjection here, of course, means the taking in of something and the making of it into part of the self.

Emptiness and "O"

Religion and psychoanalysis move toward a shared sense of the apprehension of the highest quality of mind as object. Whether this be self as Jung thought of it or Godhead, personal or impersonal, may be merely a matter of terms. As we actually experience them we may simply be unable to differentiate clearly the human from the divine, just as we cannot distinguish the object as a thing in itself from the phenomenon as the mind constructs it.

Contemporary psychoanalysis has taken the object's primacy to development as Klein described it and brought out its duality in the internal parental couple. Of all religions, it is tantric Buddhism that anticipates this development. The importance of the couple symbolizing the object and its psychic contribution to container/ contained is reminiscent of the Oedipus complex and its dissolution. This, too, Klein (1945) anticipates in her paper on the primitive Oedipus complex.

The religious repudiation of the senses finds its equivalent in the psychoanalytic technique of abstinence. This can be seen in religion to be a matter of making room for religious experience and not just moralism This is explained by Bion in the idea of saturation and the way the senses may obscure the direct apprehension of mind.

Buddhism formulates this in the doctrine of emptiness which helps to explain Bion's idea of "O". Actually the shared realizations of psychoanalysis and Buddhism go further still in Bion's (1970, p. 30) treatment of thinking as the evolutions of "O" into K. First Meltzer's (1973) idea of the impersonality of the inner object and how he relates that to the idea of God as capable of being known not in the outer world but in the inner one is considered. Then the consideration follows Meltzer into his sense of the dual nature of the object as the internal couple and of the need for admiration if development is to take place. Corroboration of this idea is sought in the tantric Buddhist practice of the deities in embrace. In conclusion is a discussion of Bion's concept, or his empty concept, of "O" and to the precedence of the Buddhist doctrine of emptiness and particularly to the view of emptiness of Nagarjuna which is illuminated by and which illuminates projective identification.

His treatment of "O" in this way deserves extensive exegesis and personal contemplation. Finally, Bion reasserts the factor of religion in psychoanalysis when he writes:

> It may be wondered what state of mind is welcome if desire and memory are not. A term that would express approximately what I need to express is "faith"—faith that there is an ultimate reality and truth—the unknown, unknowable, "formless infinite". [*ibid.*, p. 31]

It may be that as religion passes from the exoteric belief in the unprovable to the esoteric discipline of religious experience, it ceases to be religion at all and becomes an empty concept, something we can know only by experience and cannot possess as an object of knowledge.

Notes

1. Paragraph 39 of "Notes on the theory of schizophrenia" in Bion (1967a).
2. The word "atone" was originally "at on", then "at one", and finally shortened to "atone". So much was the sense of the possibility of being "at one" lost that "to atone" came to mean "to repent". In the last century "at-one-ment" became again a possible subject and the noun atonement, sometimes with and sometimes without hyphens, began to be used in its original sense.

CHAPTER FOUR

Therapy by design: style in the therapeutic encounter

Faye Carey

Introduction

As with art, the point of psychotherapy is change. People make art, or come to it, seeking transformation—within, and without. Psychotherapy as a creative process is often compared with literature, but the comparison extends to the visual arts, too. Further, the similarity of process applies to both therapist and patient. In this chapter I consider some of the transformational or creative characteristics that these two enterprises hold in common for both participants.

In speaking of creativity I have in mind both individual originality and the ordinary inventiveness which I see as fundamental to being alive, as well as the specialized creativity we associate with art. I am looking at what the two practices, art and psychotherapy, may have in common and to this end I am thinking of the session as a creative work in its own right, with the authorship of that work shared between the patient and the therapist, each acting as both artist and audience for one another. I shall start by describing a session which I hope will bring out some of the features of the creative process which I believe these two practices hold in common.

Sam

Sam's main symptoms take the form of somatizing his feelings, with his ailments located variously in his stomach, bowel, bladder, and back. We have come to understand these complaints as both an attack on and a defence against an internalized mother who possesses and controls his body and all its functions. Those close to him find this passive form of aggression exasperating, and the somatization and hypochondria put an enormous strain on his relationships.

Two notable features mark many of his sessions: one has been my difficulty in following what Sam says. He speaks in a barely audible running mutter, full of non sequiturs. I often experience his speech as a trail of obscure clues that he has scattered in order to lose me. The second feature feels like a chronic implicit demand for praise, followed by a sense of aggrieved petulance when approval or acknowledgement does not appear to be forthcoming. In the transference he experiences me as both expectant and predictably disappointed. He links this transference experience to what appears to have been a very rigorous toilet-training, being required to be regular, clean, neat, and tidy, and a credit to his mother at all times. For my part, as well as a counter-transference sense of injustice at being attacked for judging him harshly, I also often feel as if I am being re-routed or diverted—which, at some level, is possibly what he wants, since he is as fearful as he is eager to be found. That gives something of the flavour of the sessions.

The session I describe took place shortly after a concert in which Sam was performing had to be cancelled because of his last-minute illness. This was not the first time that plans had been ruined by his ailments. The other members of the band were fed up with him.

Sam started the session with his customary inaudible mutter and fractured sentences that eventually turned out to be a report on his health, which was the cause of the ruined event and the reason the others were now furious with him. There were some threads of associations to earlier minor illnesses which had had the effect of spoiling or delaying plans. He could not understand why everyone was so unreasonably angry with him—after all, being ill wasn't his fault. He then said something about feeling deadened, and just wanting to hibernate.

I attempted to follow him through the familiar scatter of details and images: there was something about his bowel, his back, an allergy, an eye irritation, alternative medicine. Both his back and his stomach were uncomfortable, now, while lying on the couch. He then remembered a dream. And here, for the first time in the session, his words came to my ear, the trail began to clear and I found myself following him. He said "I had a dream where James and I are doing a duet. We're the hosts or presenters of some sort of programme. Somewhere in the middle of this act we have to get this man—I think it may be my [dead] brother—to do a commercial break. This brother is completely withdrawn and somehow all twisted about, physically. He was wearing a hat—I never saw his face . . . I wonder if it was really me? He was in very colourful clothes, but he was completely uncommunicative. He was wearing a long quilted sort of patchwork jacket, and a yellow and red scarf, baggy, colourful trousers. Very stagey. Very particular. He couldn't say anything, and he was in a fixed position. Paralysed. Maybe even dead. Colourful. Perfect. We tried really hard, but we couldn't get him to do the advert . . ."

The clarity and enthusiasm of his description accelerated from hesitant and uncertain to fluent and florid, and was accompanied by extravagant arm and hand gestures, alongside the striking detail—"paralysed, dead, colourful, perfect", which contrasted notably with my own internal responses to both the imagery and the narrative—as he spoke I began to hear what he was saying like a record slowing down, the sound distorting. I became aware of a low feeling, one moving in the opposite direction to his increasing animation.

I asked him what he made of this dream and he started off by saying it was very different from the recent scary dream about being chased across the desert by bandits. It appeared he wanted to tell me that there was now an improvement in the quality of his dreams—this one was more colourful, more energetic, more lively. He began to warm to the theme of improvement and upgrading: the clothes—maybe they're an expression of emotional warmth, he pondered, they were "really nice". He repeated, "Very stagey, very particular."

I said: "In your dream, you seem to be describing someone who is dead—maybe your dead brother, maybe yourself. Earlier today you said you feel 'deadened', and want to 'hibernate', and it may feel that if your brother's dead, then you have no right to life, or only one in which you're paralysed or asleep—or, possibly, one devoted to bringing him back to life?"

After a pause in which Sam appeared to be waiting, I went on: "In the dream you're trying to make this paralysed person, whom you've dressed in very 'lively' clothing, come alive—to do a TV advert. I wonder what that means to you?"

Sam said, "Do you mean what does advertising mean to me? Well," he laughed, "trying to sell something. We were quite desperate to get him—whoever he was—to perform, either for the audience, or maybe for our boss."

The precise description of the clothing—the hat, the colourful, quilted, patchwork cloak, the stripey scarf and baggy trousers—suggests a costume or disguise designed to camouflage the deadened mannequin-like form that the pair were desperately trying to revive. I say, "In the dream you are uncertain of the paralysed man's state: if he's dead, you've concealed this with lively clothing; if he's merely hibernating, you are energetically doing everything in your power to coax him back to life. Either way, it seems that his unfortunate state is your fault or your responsibility."

Sam said, "I wonder if I'm also trying to revive the dead brother for my mother." I thought this idea was reinforced by Sam's repeated use of the word "particular", which was an unusual word to use in that context, reminding me of the word "parti-coloured", which describes the apparel associated with a jester, someone who is obliged to entertain, to uplift, for a living.

I said, "You may feel you have to do that for me as well. As you were describing the dream, I felt you wanted me to hear this as a lively dream—as if you wanted not only to entertain, but to distract me with it. Distract me from the awareness that the body in the lively clothing is paralysed or possibly dead. In the dream, you are doing everything you can either to conceal this fact, or rectify it, as if someone may hold you responsible." We spoke also of the parallel between the paralysis in the dream and the paralysing back pain he'd been experiencing. Does he paralyse himself as a punishment (for the death of his brother), which has the added impact of punishing others?

Both the dream, and the way he conveyed the dream, were indicative of the style of this patient. Not only was the dream a communication concerning the nature of a disguised or concealed self, but so was Sam's initial wish to interpret, and to have me interpret, the material in a discordantly "upbeat" way—suggesting that the colour and distinctiveness were expressions of "emotional warmth"—to use his phrase—allowing him to bypass or deny the fact that the clothes were dressing a dead or paralysed man who was being forced to perform. Listening to the dream was, for me, like watching his bleak internal landscape unfold as he manically tried to grass it over. It was distressing to hear his effort to make the grotesque picturesque—as if he always had to find a way of presenting to his mother a version of himself that was acceptable, and the agony of never being able to please her was intolerable. But it is not only the unsatisfiable mother who has been internalized— the desperation in the dream to get the paralysed man to perform, to come alive, was also saying something about his inner conviction that neither his mother, nor I, could ever really forgive or welcome this murderous baby, no matter how hard he or we tried; so being himself was simply not an option available to him, in life or in the consulting room.

The creative process

This vignette helps to illustrate some of the ideas I wish to convey with regard to the role or position taken up by patient and thera- pist at different moments of the session—roles or positions that parallel those taken up by artists and the artists' materials in the creative process. The patient, through both his dream and his asso- ciations, is at first like the artist who intuitively invents some- thing—in this case, a dream. He then begins to communicate that dream, but on reflection—and here we are talking about a man who has had to become inhibited—he begins to feel he has revealed more than is safe, and so he starts to modify the work. As therapist, I feel at the start of the session as though I am confronted with a scattering of materials that need to be gathered together to see what can be made of them. Between the patient and myself a shape or pattern begins to emerge; it is as if we are both the tools and the materials. The pace and the rhythm change, there is a certain fluid- ity. The roles of artist, materials, audience begin to rotate: we are no longer simply talking about a dream, we are now involved in some- thing more like a collaborative work. This is very like the feeling when working as an artist, a slight blurring between being the author of the work, and being authored by the work. In the telling and considering of this dream, we both experienced a moment when each of us could appreciate the economy and beauty of his dream, including even the recognition of the psychic pain that it revealed.

What I wish to do here is to draw attention to the kinship of experience between the two creative practices of art and psychotherapy. Setting out to make a work of art is no guarantee of a successful outcome; the piece that you eventually stand back from may not be a work of art, but it is certainly a work: a work of exploration (I would say exploration of desire), discovery, and self-knowledge. So it is with the session. The way the artist works, the way his or her internal world is represented, and then read by the audience, can be usefully compared with the interaction between patient and therapist; the similarities may be inevitable since, I believe, these interactions may derive from a common source.

If the creative impulse is not extraordinary, but fundamental, ubiquitous, and essential to being alive, then there is something that resembles the artist both in the patient and in the therapist, and traces of the artistic process in the interpersonal encounter of the therapeutic session. Since I believe that creativity is not a secondary, but a fundamental, component of survival, and since both partners in that encounter have survived to this point, I am assuming that they have both experienced the urge, wish, or need to make something, or more accurately to make something happen, to transform, whether internally, or externally—this is what I am calling creativity. But it is not only the need to make something: it is the need to make something, or have it made, satisfactorily, in a particular way—this is what I am here calling aesthetics. In all, this contributes to a sense of style, which applies to the therapist, to the patient, and to the session. Aesthetics are often discussed as an aspect of highly refined sensory and intellectual processes. I am regarding aesthetics as a fundamental cornerstone of our emotional life and style as its expression. It will be obvious, therefore, that I understand style not as something superficial, but as something as fundamental as a signature—however stylized that may be. In making this comparison between artistic and analytic practice, I have in mind terms that are conventionally associated with the visual arts through the language of form: these include such physical formal elements as frame or boundary, medium, composition, colour, shape, pattern, dimension, scale; or the more dynamic formal elements such as colour (again), pace, rhythm, line, as well as such linguistic (but still visual) formal elements as narrative, symbol, metaphor, and so forth, all of which serve to establish and communicate ideas, concepts, moods or feelings that may be shared by artist (patient or therapist) and audience (patient or therapist), beyond the use of words—or indeed silences. As with visual art, *how* something is being expressed frames, complicates, enriches, and occasionally clarifies *what* is being expressed, particularly—for instance—when the style contradicts or challenges the content. And, of course, some of these terms have their clear counterparts in the therapeutic session, as expressed through the setting and the language of psychoanalysis, and as present in the minds and imaginations of the two people involved, and in their relationship.

Creative impulse

In assuming that the creative capacity is there virtually from the outset, I am drawing a distinction between this capacity (which I feel predates anything as sophisticated as, for example, the "depressive position") and the more developed and complex use to which this creativity may be put, which may include the need to restore or repair something lost or damaged, within the self, or the other, or both. So I am of the view that creativity is not in itself pathological, although the uses to which it can be put, or the way in which it develops or is thwarted from development, might well be. This earlier primitive impulse is linked, I imagine, quite simply to survival, a piece of inherited human diversity which has developed successfully to sustain us in our particular environments, whether friendly or hostile. This is not the creativity born of loss and mourning, but has more to do with the experience of absence in the face of need or desire, and so is connected to an impulse to invent what is not there, but is wanted. This capacity may be stimulated or enhanced by the early experience of having something appear "just when it was needed", in Winnicott's (1971) terms, ". . . as when a baby creates an object but the object would not have been created as such if it had not already been there." This I see as the forerunner of imagination: to have a sense of what *might* be, on the basis either of what is wanted, or what has been: learning to anticipate, and perhaps even influence, the future on the basis of past experience. This is the bond between experience and prediction, or between memory and prophecy. As such, this capacity is a first act of imagination: the invention in the internal world, by means of mental substitution, of the absent object of desire. We know that infants dream: what could they be dreaming about?

Winnicott (*ibid.*) describes this creativity as a "universal [which] belongs to being alive . . ." It can be distorted by environments, but cannot be destroyed utterly since it is original to the human being. He acknowledges the importance of Klein's (1957) concepts of reparation, restitution, and guilt in relation to the further development of creativity, but not in relation to the source of creativity itself. This he sees as innate, although prone to subsequent modification through either environmental or internal factors. These two aspects of creativity—the primitive impulse and the more developed response arising from conflictual experience—are components of both artistic and analytic processes. Several writers have discussed this inventive component of creativity as contrasted with its reparative aspect. In "The nature and function of phantasy", Susan Isaacs (1948) refers to the imaginative play that enables the child to use its past to recreate the conditions it requires to meet its present needs. Again, this refers to the experience of replacing, or inventing, what is not there, as opposed to restoring what has been damaged: a capacity significant for the creative artist, as well as for the development of a sense of reality, of scientific enquiry, and, as Isaacs says, of the "growth of hypothetical reasoning". So, once again, this creative capacity is fundamental to being alive and alert.

Reparative drives and symbol formation

> "There is no limit to how complicated things can get, on
> account of how one thing is always leading to another."
>
> E.B. White (American humorist, d. 1985).

Having acknowledged innate sources of creativity, we may consider how this capacity develops under the influence of both internal and external conditions, including now the growing need to consider the object, and to communicate. Melanie Klein (1930) precisely delineated the way in which the creative impulse is used to restore and protect the damaged object, describing at the same time the process of symbol formation. She agreed with Jones (1916) who, in his seminal work on symbol formation, held that the pleasure principle allowed for different things to be equated through "a similarity marked by gratification, enjoyment or interest", but Klein extended the associations to those subject also to anxiety. She carefully tracks the development of symbol formation, showing how the infant can spare its object from both its intense aggression and its dangerous desire. However, what I am saying is that the infant is already an old hand at this, it already has some job experience here as it learned to do this before, all those months, weeks, or moments ago, when it had to cope with absence by using—or perhaps more accurately, creating—its imagination; it already knows the useful, and reasonably reliable, trick of substituting an internal image for the absent object. And now this act of imaginative replacement can be applied to the new situation, to relieve the anxiety aroused, not now so much from absence, but from fear of potentially mutual damage and depletion. Again, through a chain of associations, it can inventively repair and restore its damaged object.

Klein follows Ferenczi in suggesting that this series of earliest associations belongs to the conflictual feelings associated with the infant's own body and that of its mother, which demand that attention be transferred from lovingly or hatefully cathected objects to initially neutral objects. However, by association, these objects themselves become newly charged and dangerous, forging an ever-extending chain of associations or symbols, linked through love and hate. Using symbol formation, the child's interest in the external world is propelled by this series of displacements. In this construction, symbol formation is associated now with a different kind of loss, one that does not assume magical replacement—the gratifyingly simple invention of the missing object, as in the earlier version—but suggests a recognition and acceptance of loss and mourning, and of—if not impotence—then at least of non-omnipotence. This is a different kind of creativity, as it requires a form of acknowledgement, having to relinquish something, and having to establish new connections. It is not magic—it is work. Creative work, like the making of art. (Creative artists not only recognize, acknowledge, and "quote" from their antecedents, but often take pleasure in that identification, even when diverging from or challenging it, as in Picasso's Las Meniñas series, or Francis Bacon's paintings of Pope Innocent, both inspired by the genius of Velasquez; or in Bill Viola's video reinvention of the *Tormenting of Christ*; or the Chapman Brothers' restaging of Goya's *The Disasters of War* with mutilated shop dummies, etc.)

It seems worth emphasizing that there is both a correlation and a distinction between the creativity that has its roots in impulse and desire, and the creativity that develops with experience: the first suggesting "lost and found", and the second implying "lost and mourned". Further, although the process of symbol formation may take place through a series of displacements, the eventual symbol is far richer than a simple substitution; the associations are non-linear: they travel dimensionally, in both space and time, and this enables expansive imaginative thinking, connections, and imagery, of both conscious and unconscious varieties, to be brought to poetry, to art, or to the session—and by both participants: artist and audience, patient and therapist alike.

Pleasure (aesthetics)

This expansion of one's sensual and cognitive universe is not at all neutral, but charged with risk and excitement. It can afford intense pleasure—a pleasure which often accompanies creativity since, alongside the anxiety attached to the original object, there is also often excitement and gratification in finding the apt substitute, the relief that what has been sought has been found; a gap has been filled, and if the process is creative, then more than filled—it is transformed into something new. Both in psychoanalysis and in art there is a searching for the specific and the apt, which corresponds to the thing we have been looking for, and which yields that satisfaction we call aesthetic pleasure. Pleasure is an important component of creativity, but it is not simple. I have a patient who is a sculptor, who works compellingly rather than compulsively, and loves doing what he does, but at the same time finds it unbearable and even humiliating when he works, or exhibits his work, as he feels naked and exposed. But while he works he is utterly absorbed, and the difficult feelings do not prevent him from working as they are continually mitigated by equally intense satisfactions. The difficulties are not avoided, but confronted in a way that can be at once frightening, stimulating, and gratifying. Thus Wordsworth describes the pleasure of creation as "the sense of difficulty overcome" and as "a complex feeling of delight, which is of the most important use in tempering the painful feeling always found intermingled with powerful descriptions of the deeper passions" (Wordsworth, 1876, p. 96).

Gilbert Rose (1987), who writes about the making and experiencing of works of art, speaks of this feeling as a sense of wholeness, suggesting that both psychoanalytic and aesthetic experiences provide an opportunity in their different ways for the integration of thought, feeling, perception, and memory through overcoming various forms of splitting. This integration can clearly be healing, and certainly contributes to the feeling of pleasure: a sense of wholeness.

It becomes clear that meaning and pleasure are closely related, a variation on Keats's equation of truth with beauty. I think the imprint of these early aesthetic experiences is deep, pervasive, and evident throughout our lives, bearing the traces of the joy and pain, or "the agony and the ecstasy", of our earliest moments. Marion Milner (1952), in speaking of the need to find a word to describe "the emotional experience of finding the substitute", indeed suggests that the word "ecstasy" would be apt. Whatever the word used, the feeling that is being described is one of satisfaction when anticipation, expectation, and event or object come together in a particularly unexpected way, so that expectations are exceeded; there is a synaptic quality, and the whole becomes greater and more surprising than the sum of its parts. (Here, however, I think, we are also entering the realm of Freud's "uncanny" and the experience can also be unnerving and unsettling.)

I think that grasping something of this synaptic process is fundamental to understanding how things become beautiful for us—another way of describing the aesthetic moment which applies to art, science, and transformational moments in the analytic session. This bringing of ideas together to form a new shape, a new concept—or "insight"—is as familiar to science as it is to art and in both is often described as "beautiful".

Recently a patient said, "I realize that I've been feeling better for some time, and I think it's because I've been able to make connections for the first time. It's not that I've discovered anything new, I've always known these things separately inside me; but I couldn't make it come together—I needed to say it out loud in order to see it." I would add that he needed to say it aloud in order to have it heard; he needed an audience, to witness together with him his internal world.

I think I am also describing the origins of a sense of form. Both the experience of having one's needs met, and the imaginative work that must be done when they are not, contribute to the development of a sense of something that contains, or that is self-containment, which in turn establishes a sense of form or cohesive shape: a capacity for meaning, and for the communication of meaning.

Within the setting of a session, I feel that I am watching out for the shape that the material is taking and either finding this form from within the material that the patient brings, or sharing it with the patient who has found it for her or himself.

I am emphasizing that aesthetics, like symbol formation, starts with the body—specifically the body of the mother, both inside and out. As the first ego is a body ego, and the first symbols symbolize the body, it is possible to understand the first aesthetic as a body aesthetic.

Meltzer, who I think has written most precisely about this, traces the perception of beauty back to the inherent endowments of the mother, as first perceived by the infant. This includes experience of the time in the womb—movement and stillness, rhythm and contrast, harmonious and agitated states, both physical and emotional, within both mother and embryo, and then the time beyond the womb, with the infant's attention centring fundamentally on both the face and the breast, their physical attributes, composition, symmetry, relationship of parts, shape, texture, shadows, temperature, planes and curves, as well as—most importantly—on responsiveness and the capacity of the breast "to restore the objects of psychic reality for the baby" (Meltzer, 1967, p. 28). (Here, I would include the eyes, the arms, and the voice in this capacity for restoration.) This sense of rightness or aptness of response lays the foundation for authenticity, or truth, and is therefore the place where truth and that which comes to be understood as beautiful, may first coincide.

However, the perception of beauty must also incorporate the idea that the object becomes truly meaningful only when it is understood that it can be lost: the object of desire is, by definition, elusive—precisely, the object that is not there. It is an unpossessable possession, which Meltzer identifies as the source of the aesthetic conflict. Things become beautiful for us in the deepest sense when we have understood the likelihood, indeed, the inevitability, of their loss.

The internal audience

In the context of this understanding of the personal and the interpersonal world of the infant we may see that through internalization and through both conscious and unconscious imagination an internal audience begins to take shape an "other" to whom the self speaks, a representation of the environment, which also includes the self. This internalization clearly embraces, but I think also exceeds, the idea of the superego as critic and censor, as it also represents the world of ideas and possibilities. The internal audience is vital to the artist, and may be what is sometimes described, or experienced, as the "muse".

I am referring often to processes that seem to take place on the threshold of in and out, internal and external, as well as of conscious and unconscious. It is primarily in this area of exchange or interchange that creativity takes place, including spontaneous discovery and invention, as well as humour. This continual to and fro between primary and secondary process provides the fundamental material of psychotherapy. It establishes a rhythm—one of the most basic but least described experiences of the analytic session. Rhythm says a lot about the internal world of the patient, and does much to establish the degree of intimacy or separation between patient and therapist. Pulse precedes mind. Rhythm sustains us prior to our entry into the world, establishing a permanent bond between time and form. It ushers us into the world and provides the background beat for all our actions and relation-ships—being born, waking, resting, and feeding, movement and gesture; the iambic pentameter of our speech and—in psychother-apy—the trace of all of these as expressed in the interchange of feelings to and fro in the shared speech and silences of the session.

Regression in the service of the ego: sublimation and inhibition

A further shared characteristic of both art and psychotherapy is the capacity to use and tolerate regression. Both require a kind of psychic unbuttoning and an ability to inhabit a somewhat childlike state, where the individual can be liberated from the constraints of logic, enabling sublimation, a central dynamic of creative activity.

Klein suggests that it is the peculiar condensation of phantasies involved in the processes of symbolization which provides the wealth of material represented in sublimation; the development of an interest in art or of a creative talent would partly depend on such condensations. When anxiety is excessive, however, creative activ-ity becomes inhibited and, if it takes place at all, it is more to please or placate. Equally likely, excessive anxiety may lead simply to inhi-bition in place of creativity, or some other displacement symptom may form. This close relationship between inhibition and sublima-tion is perhaps one of the reasons for the concern often expressed by artists that analysis will supplant—or "cure"—their creativity.

Style

Bringing all these elements together contributes to what I experi-ence as the "style" of a patient and the parallels with the style of an artist. For some artists, subject matter is a pretext for exploring subtext, for example, landscape as an exploration of the body, or still life as an exploration of the objects and relationships of the internal world. For others, subject matter is the material: narrative painting in which form and content work in harmony, as, for exam-ple, in religious paintings that express spiritual devotion. In some forms of visual art, the medium and the material are expressive of relationships, experiences, or psychological states, whereas elsewhere the work is "concrete": a statement of the actuality of the material, the thing in itself, and symbolism is eschewed. Some artists will create paradox through contrast—a lively scene in sombre tones—or, conversely, a grim subject cheerfully depicted (as with my patient). Others will pursue dreams of perfection and, through the language of purism, for example, endeavour to deny chaos. By contrast, an inhibition, or even a scepticism about clarity, may result in a picturesque clutter. No two artists work alike, but I think that many artists work *by* working, by responding to the work in front of them as if within a dialogue. A mark goes down, a move is made, another is called for in response. There is a continuing wordless conversation, when things are going well, between internal and external, as represented through the work—an experience of, or in, transitional space. At some point, it is as if the work is making the artist. Something similar, it seems to me, happens in the analytic encounter and it is not always possible to say who is the author.

These moves and moments apply not just to utterances in the session, but also to the way that patient rings or knocks, enters the room, puts down his belongings, makes contact or not; inhabits the space, speaks or remains silent, chooses his words. They apply to the rhythm, pace, tone, volume, and variety of the patient's speech, the manner of listening, or cutting off, or cutting out—all of these being the clinical counterparts of the formal components referred to above: pace, rhythm, scale, colour, composition, texture, narrative, symbol, and so forth, all held within the frame or boundary of the session and all building an impression of the style of the patient, much as the style of the artist is expressed through his or her processes and revealed in the work.

CHAPTER FIVE

Narcissism, the mystics' remedy

Josephine Klein

> "Grant, I may not like puddle lie
> In a corrupt security,
> Where, if a traveller water crave,
> He finds it dead, and in a grave;
> But as this restless, vocal spring
> All day and night doth run, and sing,
> And, though here born, yet is acquainted
> Elsewhere, and flowing keeps untainted;
> So let me all my busy age
> In thy free services engage . . ."
>
> Vaughan, "The Dawning", 1622–1695

And in this century,

> "As for the spirit of poverty, I do not remember any moment
> when it was not in me, although only to that unfortunately
> small extent which is compatible with my imperfection. I fell
> in love with St. Francis of Assisi as soon as I came to know
> about him. I always believed and hoped that one day Fate
> would force upon me the condition of vagabond and beggar

which he embraced freely. Actually I felt the same way about prison"

Weil, 1950, p. 31

Just now a circular from the Salvation Army comes through the door to remind us that every Salvation Army Officer, on being commissioned, promises

for Christ's sake, to care for the poor, feed the hungry, clothe the naked, love the unlovable, and befriend the friendless.

Narcissism

Fresh spiritual movements have always had people who become uncomfortable at being situated at the centre of their personal universe. They do not want a preoccupation with esteem, money, goods, even family, to obscure their joy in the ineffable. They fear anything that might threaten this vital connection, and one threat, in the language of the pychotherapists, is the gratification of narcissistic needs, even if these needs are generally regarded as legitimately gratifiable.

Narcissism is marked by an inability to love. People with strong narcissistic trends have to struggle to love themselves or others, have no sense of being lovable, cannot allow themselves to be loved. In a narcissistic state of mind, only one thing is deeply and immediately experienced: what happens to oneself. Some people, finding that this is how they are, do not like it. No wonder that some writings on mystical experiences read like manuals on how to counteract one's narcissistic ways or, as it used to be phrased, how to deny the self, or lose the self.

Buber gives an account of a childhood event that shows how a moment's self-preoccupation broke a boy's sense of mystical connectedness.

When I was eleven years of age, spending the summer on my grandparents' estate, I used, as often as I could do it unobserved, to steal into the stable and gently stroke the neck of my darling, a broad dapple-grey horse. It was not casual delight but a great, certainly friendly, but also deeply stirring happening. If I am to explain it now, beginning from the still very fresh memory of my hand, I must say that what I experienced in touch with the animal was the Other, the immense otherness of the Other, which, however, did not remain strange like the otherness of the ox and the ram, but rather let me draw near and touch it. When I stroked the mighty mane, sometimes marvellously smooth-combed, at other times just as astonishingly wild, and felt the life beneath my hand, it was as though the element of vitality itself bordered on my skin, something that was not I, was certainly not akin to me, palpably the other, not just another, really the Other itself; and yet it let me approach, confided itself to me, placed itself elementally in the relation of *Thou*-and-*Thou* with me. The horse, even when I had not begun by pouring oats for him in the manger, very gently raised his massive head, ears flicked, then snorted quietly, as a conspirator gives a signal meant to be recognised only by his fellow-conspirator; and I was approved. [Buber, 1947, p. 41]

Then a moment's narcissistic self-consciousness appeared, and spoiled the experience.

But once—I do not know what came over the child, at any rate it was childlike enough—it struck me about the stroking what fun it gave me, and suddenly I became conscious of my hand. The game went on as before, but something had changed, it was no longer the same thing. And the next day, after giving him a rich feed, when I stroked my friend's head, he did not raise his head . . . [*ibid.*, pp. 41–42]

Buber contends that if one is too conscious of what one is doing, as if one were watching oneself on a stage or in a novel, important elements of the experience are lost: it has dwindled into a narcissistic experience. Buber calls the moment of narcissistic self-consciousness *reflexion*, which felicitously suggests that it is a moment of watching oneself as in a mirror. He also suggests that it is a moment when other people and things lose their quiddity.

. . . when a man withdraws from accepting with his essential being another person in his particularity . . . and lets the other exist only as his experience, only as "a part of myself" . . . then dialogue becomes a fiction, the mysterious intercourse between two human worlds only a game, and in the rejection of the real life confronting him, the essence of all reality begins to disintegrate. [*ibid.*, p. 43]

In practice, narcissism may be seen as a difficulty in experiencing other people as having an existence of their own, with their own inner world, with a capacity for suffering and joy in their own way independent of our needs or our views on the matter. Narcissism prevents us from relating to others in such a way that their sorrows and joys can cause us sorrow or joy except by way of envy.

Some developmental antecedents of adult narcissism

Some well-intentioned self-centred people hate themselves, turning against the whole experience of having a self. This is rather different from the more common resolution to set one's face against what one fears may hinder the possibility of joy, bliss or goodness—the possibility of having a good object within, psychotherapists might say. Those who really hate themselves wrestle with anxiety and guilt about the selfish elements they notice in their every action, and that makes life very hard for them. Gerard Manley Hopkins (1844–1889) writes about this unhappy situation:

> I see
> The lost are like this, and their scourge to be,
> As I am mine, their sweating selves; but worse.
> [Hopkins, 1885, "I wake and feel the fell of dark"]

and

> My own heart let me more have pity on; let
> Me live to my sad self hereafter kind,
> Charitable; not live this tormented mind
> With this tormented mind tormenting yet.
> [ibid., "My own heart let me more have pity on"]

Such people do not want to be as they are; they dislike themselves, their desires and phantasies feel too powerful to be contained by ego and superego. Maybe they were born more passionate than the norm? Maybe their normal-strength childhood impulses were not handled well by those who took care of them? Maybe something went wrong at the point where the infant's naturally rather autistic narcissism had to be abandoned for the reality-principles that rule the world we share with others.

Differences in the degree of pathological narcissism must be attributable, at least in part, to differences in the way people's healthy narcissism was respected in childhood. If their littleness and dependence was taken into account, so that they found their grownups helpful rather than scornful, all may be well. But those whose littleness was used to make them feel needy, negligible, or exploited, may not find it easy to like other people's power, good fortune, goodness, richness. Fortunate children grow up into people who do not feel ashamed at being imperfect, at not being omnipotent. They are pleased that there is someone else who can be perfect. There is less envy. There are babies who had terrific fun when they were learning to use a spoon to eat with, who were allowed to push the goo into the mouth of whoever was willing to accept the stuff—a diagram of mutual pleasure-giving.

The proviso is—you must not be too hungry: Kohut writes that psychotherapists interpret appropriately in terms of drive-theory only when patients have been too damaged by deprivation or excess to be able to form gratifying object-relations (Kohut, 1977, Ch. 2, esp. pp. 86–88). The more fortunate children will have been able to learn that it is almost as pleasant to hand out sweeties as to eat them yourself; something unhappy must have already happened to a child that feels it must have all the toffees. What fun to put socks on your baby brother's feet—if you don't feel deprived of parental care yourself.

Those unfortunates who did not learn the pleasures of exchange at the right time have more problems with greed, envy, selfishness, and such. They are in conflict much of the time, and have to make grand unnatural gestures. If they want to be good, they long to be hermits or martyrs in order to keep themselves from falling back into the greed and selfishness they dislike so much. More moderate fallible people apologise and are forgiven and received back into the fallible circle where they did their damage, as the Count does at the end of *The Marriage of Figaro*, and Baron Ochs at the end of the *Rosenkavalier*, when the Marschallin also acknowledges her limitations. In the same vein are the moving reconciliations—improbable as they may be—at the end of *A Winter's Tale*.

At its best, the anti-narcissistic training recommended by many mystics is a training in getting into a mental attitude that is not easily destroyed by the knowledge of one's imperfection.

Via negativa and narcissism

The literature on mysticism shows two main approaches to the ineffable, depending among other things on how people feel about being the kind of person they are. Of course, much of what is written is a mixture of the two approaches—not always compatibly but that is the nature of the material, few mystics being logicians.

Via negativa recommends the systematic eradication of the self from the centre of action and consciousness. From this perspective, the self is regarded not as what you naturally live and love with, but as a hindrance to loving others and a hindrance to the source from which love flows. *Via negativa* is likely to be the self-prescription of people who feel plagued by their narcissism; they dislike being as they are.

> It comes to this, that we must surrender all that is dearest to us in the enjoyment of the senses and go through a dark night in which we live without their help and comfort. Then when this is accomplished we have to sacrifice the prerogative of our own way of thinking and willing, and undergo another still darker night in which we have deprived ourselves of all the supports which are familiar to us and make us self-sufficient. This is a kind of death, the making nothing of all that we are to ourselves; but the genuine mystic tells us that when all has been strained away our emptiness will be filled with a new presence; our uncovered soul will receive the contact of divine love . . . [D'Arcy, 1951 p. 6]

Via negativa comes in two fairly respectable versions, plus some that may be regarded as perverse. One respectable version maintains that there is a God, or there is a life-style of ineffable value, so other that no gratifying encounter with it is available to ordinary people with ordinary senses and ordinary shortcomings. From this it is an easy step to believing that ordinary people need not apply. D'Arcy is a relatively sympathetic twentieth-century proponent of this view.

The second version of *via negativa*, also respectable, comes from the idea that we are so preoccupied with other interests that we do not notice or do not recognize bliss even when it is all around us. " 't is ye, 't is your estrangèd faces, that miss the many-splendoured thing" wrote the Edwardian Francis Thompson in "In no strange land". Seventeenth-century George Herbert has quite a few poems about not chasing glory, wit, social life, and so on, because God is more worth having. And at times a notion also creeps in that there is something intrinsically meritorious about "sacrificing" these things.

> Lord, in my silence how I do despise
> What upon trust
> Is stylèd honour, riches, or fair eyes
> But is but dust!
>
> [Herbert, "Frailty"]

At the healthier end of the spectrum, what we are here considering is our difficulty in loving anything singled-heartedly for very long if it does not give continuous satisfaction. Most of us can accept, with greater or lesser reluctance, that this seems to be how we are constituted, but people who believe that there is nothing more worth while than loving God at all times may find it distressing to discover how little time they spend in loving anyone at all. If they are ambitious to get closer to ineffable glory, and find that love does not come easy, they may recruit for this purpose whatever pushy muscle has proved successful in other aspects of their life, and then they may get very near to perverted ideas of holiness. For instance, the fourteenth-century author of *The Cloud of Unknowing*, usually very acceptable to modern minds, starts off with a dissertation on the value of obedience and doing as one is told, in keeping with the ethos of the feudal system in which he grew up, but he occasionally gets carried over the top in a surprisingly neurotic-sounding style.

> Try to suppress all knowledge and feelings of anything less than God, and trample it down deep under the cloud of forgetting ...
> For it is the way of the perfect lover not only to love what he loves more than himself, but also in some sort to hate himself for the sake of what he loves. [*The Cloud of Unknowing* Ch.43]

John Donne (1573–1631), generally a man of strong feelings, can indulge in quite violent phantasies of overcoming narcissistic inclinations.

> Batter my heart, three-person'd God: for, you
> As yet but knock, breathe, shine, and seek to mend;

That I may rise, and stand, o'erthrow me, and bend
Your force, to break, blow, burn, and make me new.

[Sonnet vi]

Not being a twentieth-century man, he can move unselfcon-
sciously into a quite explicitly masochistic mode later in the poem.

Take me to you, imprison me, for I
Except you enthrall me, never shall be free,
Nor ever chaste, except you ravish me.

[*ibid.*]

The routinization of charisma

When we turn from the wilder extremes of *via negativa*, we can find
people who regard self-centredness more calmly as a misfortune
that can be remedied by good management, the wish to amend,
good will, reason, a sense of proportion and other rather appealing
virtues of the Age of Enlightenment. Such qualities can also be
taken to extremes, but those who possess them are attractive when
contrasted with their more excitable and dramatizing compeers. On
the other hand, those who have had to struggle against their own
urgent narcissistic inclinations may at times find such complacency
grating.

The term "routinization of charisma" was coined by Max Weber
at the start of the twentieth century, and came into prominence
among English-speaking sociologists through the translating and
editing work of C. Wright Mills and H. H. Gerth in mid-century.
The routinization or bureaucratization of charisma denotes a stage
in the process of social change, when change is initiated by remarkable personalities who have a gift for making what they advocate
sound convincing to the general populace or to groups in power;
major changes may then come about in belief-systems, the distrib-
ution of social goods, and the position of social groups relative to
one another (Gerth & Mills, 1948). Weber (1908) called people who
do this kind of thing "charismatic leaders", since it was by their
charisma—the word means grace, but carried for Weber a connota-
tion of irresistible appeal—that these amazing changes came about.
Weber considered that often, when these leaders aged or died, there

would remain a set of devoted adherents who were by their nature followers and not innovators. They would tidy up the inconsistencies in their leader's pronouncements as these became apparent, and ensure that no one would deviate unknowingly from what had been revealed to them. This is the process Weber called the routinization or the bureaucratization of charisma. It is a term that easily comes to mind when reading some mystics' and theologians' material, and it may be seen as a perversion of healthier attempts to keep narcissism within limits.

We know this, but nevertheless seem often tempted into definitions and prescriptions on how to live. If we look at eighteenth-century William Law's *Serious Call to a Devout and Holy Life*, we may indeed think for a while that if we could but follow his advice on how to pray—what to focus on at the sixth hour (gratitude and joyful devotion), what at the ninth hour (humility) and so on—we might be safe from narcissism once and for all. How sensible and practical he is, suggesting when we should pray, how, about what, when to praise, when to intercede for others, and, incidentally, how to educate both girls and boys. All in his adult ego- and superego-based way, and of course inevitably in danger of routinization and of the amazing lack of imaginativeness that so often accompanies bureaucratic solution:

> By love, I do not mean any natural tenderness, which is more or less in people according to their constitutions; but I mean a larger principle of the soul, founded in reason and piety, which makes us tender, kind and benevolent to all our fellow creatures as creatures of God, and for his sake.

> It is this love, that loveth all things in God, as His creatures, as the images of His power, as the creatures of His goodness, as part of His family, as members of His society, that becomes a holy principle of all great and good actions. [Law, 1728, Ch. 20]

However true and worthy this statement, it is a little chilling. What we may call the Holy-Living Party needs a wary as well as a sympathetic eye. The excesses of bureaucratic formulation about what is right and how to live in all eventualities (all eventualities tending to be regarded as potentially morally threatening) can kill good feelings. However, in the climate prevailing at the time of writing, we are equally in danger from the anything-goes-as-long-as-you're-sincere-and-don't-think party.

Holy living, or even just living in a happy harmless friendly social way with a proper concern for others, may be possible for long stretches of time if there have been long stretches of happiness in childhood that still resonate in the adult's unconscious processes. Otherwise, like the depressive position, it can be rather tiring and, in its pathological form, severe and sado-masochistic. On the other hand, if there is too little moral earnestness, too little encouragement to develop adult ways and concentrate the mind on reason, and evaluate and plan ahead, we get babyish ways.

Holy silliness as an anti-bureaucratic anti-obsessional remedy for narcissism

In the Table of Contents of *The Little Flowers of St. Francis of Assissi*, who lived from 1181 to 1226, we find

> *Chapter Three:* How St. Francis, having allowed an evil thought to arise in his mind against Brother Bernard, ordered him to place his foot three times upon his neck and his mouth . . .

> *Chapter Eleven:* How St. Francis made Brother Masseo turn round and round like a child, then go to Siena . . .

> *Chapter Twenty-One:* Of the most holy miracle of St. Francis in taming the fierce wolf of Gubbio. [St Francis of Assissi, 1926]

The wolf, writes the author, after hearing St Francis preach, ate only vegetables for the rest of its life; it was fed by the charity of the townspeople of Gubbio, and it followed St Francis everywhere.

Part Two of *The Little Flowers* is about Brother Juniper, and uncritically reports him as acting much dafter than St Francis and, it may be thought, with less point. For instance, one of the brothers was very ill and in his fever longed for some pork. So Juniper hurried away and cut the leg off a local live pig so that his brother might have some pork. The owner of the pig is furious and shouts at Juniper.

> Brother Juniper, who delighted in insults, cared nothing for all this abuse but, marvelling that anyone should be wroth at what seemed

to him only a matter for rejoicing, he thought he had not made himself well understood, and so he repeated the story over again, and then flung himself on the man's neck and embraced him, telling him that all had been done out of charity, and inciting him and begging him for the rest of the swine also; and all this with so much charity, simplicity and humility, that the man's heart was changed within him.

So off went the owner, killed the pig and gave it to the friars.

Then St. Francis, considering the simplicity and patience under adversity of this good brother Juniper, said to his companions and those who stood by: "Would to God I had a forest of such Junipers."

What remedies are there for narcissism?

Bureaucratic rules and holy silliness are extreme self-help solutions to the problems of narcissism, but people may be drawn to them by the dilemma in which they feel caught. For one may feel grand and in control in the confident narcissistic mode but, nagging at the threshold of consciousness, there is also the depressing knowledge that one is not permanently perfect. Yet behind every cry deploring one's inadequacy lies also a hidden conviction of unacknowledged potential. Neither the wretchedness nor the grandeur can be felt quite sincerely. Narcissism is a delusional state.

In their obsessive preoccupation with perfection and imperfection, people may resort to extreme measures to get rid of the self. They flinch from other people and isolate themselves because of their shame and guilt and fear, or they protect themselves with rules that disregard their many harmless needs or, resorting to holy silliness, make fun of the whole predicament, like the punks. No wonder that ever since the trait was first delineated, narcissism has proved difficult to modify, either through psychoanalytically-based talking-cures or through other therapeutic measures.

Via negativa advocates repression and superego control. The problem then is that with these agencies at the centre of personality organization, the self is the focus of attention. That is no way of getting rid of obsession with the self: struggling by these means to eradicate the self, we fall from self-absorption into self-obsession.

Can self-forgetfulness work? It is much commended by the mystics. But people with pathological narcissism cannot forget themselves; they are compelled by their distresses to take themselves too seriously. Self-acceptance first, then? But self-acceptance, that healthy-minded prescription, cannot work if people cannot forget themselves. Presumably, not having felt accepted by those who took care of them in earlier days, they cannot accept themselves as they are now, nor can they accept other people as *they* are now without anger, shame or guilt. If they could accept the facts of good and bad intermixed, they might be able to forget and, for a while at least, live with their imperfections and sometimes downright nastinesses without obsessing about them.

In the quaint language of psychoanalysis—no more quaint than the language of the mystics, though—there are three great realities we deny at our peril. They were first enunciated by Money-Kyrle (1971) and brought back into more general circulation by John Steiner (1993). In this more recent version, the three great realities we want to deny, but deny at our peril, are the goodness of the breast, the sexual intercourse of our parents, and our mortality. These three considerations freeze the blood in our narcissistic veins:

● we depend on others for our survival
● we did not create ourselves, and the people on whom we depend do not exist just for us but have interests apart from us
● everything and everyone must die and eventually come to an end.

To anticipate our final conclusion, what appears essential is that there should be someone of importance who is willing to put up with the narcissistic tiresomenesses of the person in distress; what is needed is someone who continues to believe unsentimentally in the other person's potential for good, when there appears little evidence of it. This must be someone whose well-being is ultimately independent of what the sufferer is up to—it must not be a spouse, a parent or child or too devoted friend, or anyone who is at risk of being personally implicated—"co-dependent" is the current term—lest their involvement adds to the narcissistic person's guilt or shame or sense of importance. The fate of this helpful figure must not be entirely in the hands of the sufferer.

Culture clashes

The mystics, those psychotherapists of earlier days, contribute something to the discussion of narcissism that is not totally new to the modern mind but highlights some aspects that might otherwise not be seen in their full significance. The misdeeds for which their culture is responsible may tempt us to turn away, and the language is often unfamiliar, based as it it is on a different view of what life is about, but if we are to learn from the experiences of people from another culture, we have to overcome the embarrassment or antagonism (or sentimental idealized attachment) we may have about that culture's language. If we do so, we may find support for some tentative modern ideas about narcissism and its remedies. In any case, remedies may be efficacious even when we do not share the assumptions (in this case Christian theological assumptions) on the grounds of which remedy is recommended. For the assumption may not affect in any relevant way the relationship between sufferer and therapist on which the remedy depends. It is possible to learn from another culture without taking it over wholesale.

Via positiva *is a remedy but . . .*

In *via positiva* people characteristically look at, or relate in some way to, a blissful other. This is what Charles Williams (1943) meant by a Beatrician moment, and the Lady Julian of Norwich by her report that the Lord

> . . . said again and again: It is I, it is I who am most exalted, it is I whom you love. It is I whom you delight in . . . It is I whom you serve; it is I whom you long for, whom you desire; it is I whom you mean; it is I who am all. [Julian of Norwich, Twelfth revelation, Ch. 26]

This would not leave a person much space for other preoccupations. *Via positiva* is a prophylactic and a remedy for narcissism; it is based on the idea that blissful communion is the most natural thing in the world. *Via positiva* does not tell people that they are wonderful or wicked, it tells them that it does not matter whether they are or not. Then they can stop obsessing. "I would beside my Lord be watching", sings the tenor in Bach's "St Matthew Passion", "And so my sin would fall asleep." That is, it will not keep him awake.

At its best, the recommended anti-narcissistic training of the mystics is a training in knowing what you are, and looking beyond that. Knowing what you are is also an avowed aim of psychotherapy—indeed, the two trainings, mystical and psychotherapeutic, have interesting elements in common, as several of the passages which follow will show.

It has to be acknowledged that these are some pre-conditions, some of which require hard work. Those fortunate people who can just forget about themselves often write as if lack of self-concern and a happily loving life are as easy as breathing, but as a regular thing it is probably only achieved after much experience of breath-management. Doubtless most of them had times when they needed to direct their attention consciously and conscientiously to the source from which they derived their sense of well-being. Very few of them can have maintained their concentration indefinitely without support. Many of them lived very disciplined lives, in their solitary hermitages, in their religious communities, amid family demands or other commitments.

There is bound to be tension between the extremes of *via positiva* and *via negativa*, between the all-you-need-is-love camp and the love-is-not-enough brigade who think that because people are easily lazy, greedy, short-sighted, etc., an internal bureaucrat needs to be installed. William Law's prescriptions usually strike a pleasant balance. Clearly in favour of internal bureaucrats, he recommends them with a verve and common sense that makes them less unattractive. His anti-narcissistic prescriptions may be summed up as, first, to establish a disciplined way of life and adhere to a routine so as to be able to resist impulses that have doubtful antecedents, and, second, to love other people in a practical way whether you feel much for them or not, and , third, to get some self-knowledge.

Lastly, you are not to content yourself with a hasty general review of the day, but you must enter upon it with deliberation, begin with the first action of the day, and proceed, step by step, through every particular matter that you have been concerned in, and so let no time, place, or action be overlooked. [Law, 1728, Ch. 23]

Self-knowledge and self-forgetfulness need each other

It will not do simply to laugh at William Law's sobriety, for the refreshing lack of interest in one's virtues and/or shortcomings, so characteristic of *via positiva*, may not endure indefinitely, just as new insights in the course of psychotherapy often seem to lose their power.

> When a man is experiencing in his spirit this nothing in its nowhere, he will find that his outlook undergoes the most surprising changes. As the soul begins to look at it, he finds that all his past sins, spiritual and physical, that he has committed from the day he was born, are secretly and sombrely depicted on it. They meet his gaze at every turn, until at last, after much hard work, many heartfelt sighs and many bitter tears, he has virtually washed them all away. [*The Cloud of Unknowing*, 1961, Ch. 69]

Psychotherapists see this as a process of "working through" an insight.

> In this interior examination you will come to recognize the honour and dignity proper to the soul at its creation, and the error and wretchedness into which you have fallen through sin. This realization will bring with it a heartfelt desire to recover the dignity and honour which you have lost. You will be filled with disgust and contempt for yourself . . . [Hilton, Book One, Ch. 42]

but also you will

> resolve to humble yourself and destroy everything that stands between you and that dignity and joy. [*ibid.*]

And then comes the interesting advice:

> However vile a wretch you are, and however great the sins you have committed, forget yourself and all that you have done, both good and bad. Ask for mercy with humility and trust. [*ibid.*,. Ch. 44]

After self-knowledge may come humility, and humility can bring self-forgetfulness.

One may note, in passing, Hilton's therapeutic respect for the typical narcissistic inflation of self-importance, "However vile you are . . .", together with the instruction that both good and bad have to be forgotten—the remedy lies in looking away from oneself.

Jakob Boehme (1970) is quoted by Florence Allshorn (1957, p. 66) as writing that "there are still deep longings in us, which hold us back from doing everything in love" and she refers to the "passions, resentments and pride" which we have to "drag into the light" so that we may "accept them, recognize their ugliness and their deep roots, desiring that no pride or fear shall blind us to our condition." We need "faith that, in bringing them to the light, they can be changed"—a belief that psychotherapists also have—and Allshorn warns that this "means death to all our carefully built-up self-esteem and self-defence" (*ibid.*, p. 66).

Boehme uses the phrase "self-naughting" to describe the process that psychotherapists call "working through": allowing oneself, in the supportive presence of another person, to find and reconsider more and more those things in oneself that make for unease and guilt or shame.

> The whole of the ascent is summed up in this "clearing of yourself" as St. Paul calls it; this "know yourself" of the saints; to discover every impulse in you of self-love and self-assertion; then to let them go into the ready helping hands of a Saviour, knowing a great self-emptying . . . [*ibid.*, p. 66]

Then

> at the root of you, instead of the old unease, the old feeling of guilt, the lovelessness, there is the constant happy shining, whatever comes, a great and smiling content. [*ibid.*, p. 67]

Dependence on a good object

Dependence on a good object is many mystics' specific remedy for narcissism; Boehme writes movingly of our need to love and be loved, and of the dreadful void left in the psyche of those whose capacity for loving and being loved has been stunted or abraded. For Boehme, that love is the natural condition of life.

> His creatures must always be desirous, because the flame of His desire entered into them at their creation. It is their energy and their elation. If they let go of Love, they let go of life and go out where darkness and death are, and have nothing but anxious and unsatisfied desires. [*ibid.*, p. 65]

> If . . . we were made to love, then every creature is desirous of find- ing this disinterested love, . . . and all the unhappiness, the struggle to make oneself felt, anger, self-assertion . . . dryness and depres- sion are only desire robbed of love. [*ibid.*, p. 65]

Here narcissism, which is an obsessive putting oneself in the centre of attention, is considered both a cause and a consequence of lack of love at the centre. People afflicted in this way cannot let go, cannot forget themselves, are compelled to take themselves seriously, in order to have a centre at all. The remedy is humility.

> Humility says "I am nothing, I have nothing." Love says "I desire only one thing, which is Jesus." [Hilton, Book Two, Ch. 21]

Via positiva relies on dependence, conscious or unconscious, on a good internal object. When we feel that ultimately all will be well because we have resources with which to meet all eventualities, it is easier to do without the immediate gratifications that greed, vindictiveness, or throbbing genitals can provide—and also with- out the consolation of despising oneself for being such a remarkable sinner. There are more hopeful ways of feeling good if we think we have access to unfailing resources. We need not at this point ask if they are located within us or elsewhere, though the old mystics had no doubts about it:

> He is our resting-place; when we come to Him we have nothing else to search for, or to desire, or to disquiet ourselves with at all; and then our soul perceives that it is has reached the haven where it would be; it has found the place where it can rest . . . In this one Good we have all that is good. [Tersteegen, 1986, letter VI]

The *via positiva* mystics point at bliss and say "look how blissful, how comforting, how good, how much love is here." "Look what fun I have", says St Francis. "Look how happy I am", says Brother Lawrence.

> And it was observed that in the greatest hurry of business in the kitchen he still preserved his recollection and heavenly-minded-ness. He was never hasty nor loitering, but did each thing in its season, with an even uninterrupted composure and tranquillity of spirit. "The time of business," said he, "does not with me differ from the time of prayer, and in the noise and clutter of my kitchen, while several persons are at the same time calling for different things, I possess God in as great tranquillity as if I were on my knees at the Blessed Sacrament." [Brother Lawrence, 1956, end of Fourth conversation]

Relationship as part of the remedy

Accept the facts; forget the fuss. It may be possible for people to forget themselves after they have faced some facts about themselves that they had been trying hard to ignore but until they can do this, one fact is that they are at times unacceptable to themselves and others, and they have to live with that. The solution suggested by these mystics is to be in a relationship with a good object, to experience being appreciated without prior conditions, to begin to feel kinship with other people who are also imperfect, eventually recognizing that they may have something you need and that you may also have something to offer.

This speaks directly to the sense of wretchedness and useless-ness against which the narcissistic hype is a defence. The more attractive *via positiva* mystics regarded narcissism as a misfortune to be managed into diminution until there was hardly any left, and , as a way of learning to manage it, they suggested self-knowledge, a cast of mind in which people get used to seeing themselves and their imperfections not alone but in company, in a relationship with others, or one Other, concerned and able to bear the inevitable dependence such a relationship creates.

Modern remedies against such obsessions as alcohol depen-dence, or other substance abuse, follow the same lines. An upbeat confident note characterizes much of their advice: if you can accept that you are as you are and that you depend on the kindness of good objects inner and outer, your obsessions will diminish. Often another person, who may also have been addicted, is provided to help you develop the capacity to be honest with yourself and with others. Believing that you can be rescued by another's efforts is good medicine for narcissism.

The same process can at times be found in the modern consulting-room, with some psychotherapists and perhaps more often with counsellors, whose training until recently tended to discourage them from too much busy-ness, for this work needs a great deal of un-oppressive patience.

From the sufferer's side there is also a proviso: an insistently self-satisfied client is an incurable one. Patients with narcissistic problems, before they can work well in therapy, require that modicum of self-knowledge or insight that tells them there is something amiss over and above their own sinfulness or the injustice of other people. But granted even just an occasional discomfort about their condition, relationship with another person becomes crucial— the rest of the requisite self-knowledge will follow later, though probably slowly. The relationship with the psychotherapist, well managed, may make possible a person's growing consciousness of narcissistically-based problems as they arise in that relationship and elsewhere, and this can then lead to increased self-understanding and acceptance.

All this is now well understood, and that makes it all the more interesting that trained professionals can still sometimes find the narcissistic personality so blindingly irritating that, famous and rightly respected though they may be, they can lose their cool, and more than a hint of annoyance can creep into their tone. Perhaps our own pressure to put the annoying patient right gets so strong that we cannot help making the relationship disagreeable to the patient, and of course the narcissistically wounded patient then becomes more tiresome than ever. Otto Kernberg's understanding and intentions are flawless when he describes, in *Severe Personality Disorders* (1984), what is likely to happen when the therapist tries to help people with strong narcissistic tendencies. For instance, a patient who has been talking about something that has engaged his or her interest, may find the therapist cuts across this with a comment that is meant to throw new light on the patient's underlying personality dynamics. By doing this, the therapist fails, as

Kernberg put it, "to fulfil the patient's expectation for admiration and reconfirmation of the grandiose self". True, though not a very nice way of putting it to the patient. Such events, Kernberg writes,

... typically evoke anger, rage, or a sudden devaluation of the analyst and his comments. Similar reactions characteristically follow times when the patient has felt important understanding and help coming from the analyst, understanding and help that painfully bring him to an awareness of the analyst's autonomous, independent functioning. The analyst's tolerance of such periods of rage or devaluation, his interpretation of the reasons for the patient's reactions, gradually permit the patient to integrate the positive and negative aspects of the transference: to integrate idealization and trust with rage, contempt, and paranoid distrust. [Kernberg, 1984, p. 198]

Even in this passage, a perhaps over-sensitive reader might be uncomfortable at the tone of Kernberg's account: no reference is made here to the pain of the dilemma facing such patients, who are required to give up, bit by bit, the habits of thinking of a lifetime, habits they have lived by, however uncomfortably. Kernberg's account is almost entirely in terms of the patient's recalcitrance. On subsequent pages, where many of the narcissistic patient's feelings are impeccably accurately described, the note of resentment is unmistakeable. Here, for instance, is part of an explanation of a patient's rage:

... periods of emptiness and the patient's feeling that "nothing is happening" in the treatment situation may often be clarified as an active, unconscious destruction of what the patient is receiving from the analyst, a reflection of the patient's inability to depend on the analyst as a giving maternal figure.

The patient's avid efforts to obtain knowledge and understanding from the analyst in order to incorporate them as something forcefully extracted rather than something received with gratitude contribute to the unconscious spoiling of what is received, a complex emotional reaction first clarified by Rosenfeld (1964) and one that usually takes a long time to resolve. Typically, lengthy periods of intellectual self-analysis, during which the patient treats the analyst as absent (which may elicit negative counter-transference in the form of boredom), are followed by or interspersed with periods when the patient eagerly expects and absorbs interpretations, attempts to outguess the analyst, rapidly incorporates what he has received as if he himself knew it all along, only once more to feel strangely empty, dissatisfied, as not having received anything after this new knowledge has been, as it were, metabolized.

By the same token, the patient typically, by projection, assumes that the analyst has no genuine interest in him, is as self-centered and exploitative as the patient experiences himself to be, and has no authentic knowledge or convictions but only a limited number of tricks and magical procedures which the patient needs to learn and incorporate. The more corrupt the patient's superego, and the more he needs to project devalued self and object representations, the more he suspects the analyst of presenting similarly corrupt and devalued characteristics. The gradual emergence or breakthrough of more primitive transferences may shift this overall picture into the expression of paranoid distrust and direct aggression in the transference. [*ibid.*]

People with narcissistic disorders need regular contact with a good-humoured therapist, who can identify with narcissistic reactions, and bear them with a warmer equanimity. This allows the sufferer gradually to be less fearful and, little by little, to let go of these unpleasant defences against self-knowledge and self-acceptance. Interestingly, it was the counselling ethic of empathic listening and unconditional acceptance, and of reflecting back without the overtones of a judgemental need to put the client right, that made it possible for some sufferers to find relief in the middle of the twentieth century, when psychoanalytic techniques were still focused almost exclusively on interpretation and the achievement of intellectual insight. Kernberg, of course, knows this. In the same book from which the above excepts were taken, different types of psychotherapy are recommended for different casts of mind, and classical psychoanalysis recommended only for people with the kind of personality-structure Kernberg thinks can bear it. (Kernberg, 1984, pp. 206 ff. and 147 ff.; see also Klein, 1995, pp. 157 ff.)

Finally: recognition

What happens in fortunate relationships with good psychotherapists not too plagued by having to protect their own narcissistic pains, is that people feel recognized and accepted. This makes possible a diminution of self-consciousness, of what Buber called "reflexion" (see p. 69). As people with narcissistic problems become more able to tolerate their imperfections because they feel recognized and accepted, there will also be a diminution in their tense fault-finding disapproval of others.

The secret ingredient, for narcissistically afflicted people as for others, is "Recognition". Recognition is the natural opposite of narcissistic loving. For narcissistic patients this means that their good qualities are seen with appreciation and pleasure, not judgementally, scornfully or spitefully. Also their own arrogance and spite are understood and respected as defences against the pain that the fear of their own imperfection inflicts on them.

The therapist may have to assume that the pain is there, for there may for a while be little evidence of this repressed or split-off-life. Not that the therapist has to conceal his or her knowledge of the patient's spiteful dealings, but if it can at all be managed, the patient must be kept secure in the therapist's recognition that he or she is a potentially whole person, whose history contains much hidden and often unconscious shame, guilt, and pain. Until these are clearly known by both patient and therapist—which requires a lot of work—the therapist cannot be fully experienced by the patient as "knowing the patient", and during this time the therapist has to accept the patient without full knowledge of all circumstances. But that seems in any case an inescapable condition of honest living.

REFERENCES

Adams, M. (2002). Dreams and the discovery of the inner world. *Journal of the British Association of Psychotherapists, 40*: 20–32.

Alexander, F. (1931). Buddhistic training as an artificial catatonia. *The Psychoanalytic Review, XVIII(2)*.

Allshorn, F. (1957). *The Notebooks of Florence Allshorn*. London: S.C.M. Press.

Astor, J. (1995). *Michael Fordham Innovations in Analytical Psychology* (Makers of Modern Psychotherapy). London: Routledge.

Balint, M. (1968). *The Basic Fault*. London: Tavistock.

Bion, W. (1959). Attacks on linking. *International Journal of Psychoanalysis, 40*: 5–6. In: *Second Thoughts*. London: Karnac, 1987.

Bion, W. (1962a). A theory of thinking. *International Journal of Psychoanalysis, 43*: 4–5. In: *Second Thoughts*. London: William Heinemann Medical Books, 1967 [reprinted London: Karnac, 1987].

Bion, W. (1962b). *Learning from Experience*. London: William Heinemann Medical Books [reprinted London: Karnac, 1984].

Bion, W. (1967a). Commentary. In: *Second Thoughts* (p. 144). London: William Heinemann Medical Books [reprinted London: Karnac, 1987].

Bion, W. (1967b) [1988]. Notes on memory and desire. In: E. Bott Spillins (Ed.), *Melanie Klein Today, Volume 2*. London: Routledge/ Tavistock].

Bion, W. (1970). Reality sensuous and psychic. *Attention and Interpretation*. London: Tavistock [reprinted London: Karnac, 1984].

Boehme, J. (1970). *The Way to Christ (and other writings)*. P.Erb (Ed./Trans.). New York: Paulist Press.

Bohm, D. (1982). The enfolding–unfolding universe. In: K. Wilber (Ed.) *The Holographic Paradigm*. Boston: Shambhala.

Bollas, C. (1987). The *Shadow of the Object*. London: Free Association Books.

Britton, R. (1998). *Belief and Imagination. Explorations in Psychoanalysis* (The New Library of Psychoanalysis). London: Routledge.

Brother Lawrence (1956). *The Practice of the Presence of God.* H. Martin (Ed.). London: S.C.N. Press.

Buber, M. (1947). *Between Man and God.* R. G. Smith (Trans.). London: Routledge & Kegan Paul.

Cloud of Unknowing (unknown fourteenth-century author) (1961). C. Wolters (Trans.) Harmondsworth. Penguin Books, 1961.

Concise Oxford Dictionary, 8th edition. Oxford: Clarendon Press.

D'Arcy, M. C. (1951). *Preface to the Poems of St. John of the Cross.* London: Harvill Press.

Devereaux, G. (Ed.) (1953). *Psychoanalysis and the Occult.* New York: International Universities Press.

Donne, J. (1572–1631). Holy Sonnet vi. In: *The Oxford Book of Christian Verse.* Oxford: Oxford University Press.

Eliot, T. S. (1961) [1922]. The Wasteland. In: *Selected Poems.* London: Faber.

Fordham, M. (1989). *The Apprehension of Beauty* [book review]. *The Journal of Analytical Psychology,* 34: 299–301.

Frazer, J. G., (1957) [1922]. *The Golden Bough.* Abridged edition. London: Macmillan.

Grinberg, L., Sor, D., & Tabak de Bianchedi, E. (1975). *Introduction to the Work of Bion.* The Roland Harris Educational Trust. [Reprinted London: Karnac Books, 1985.]

Groddeck, G. (1923). *The Unknown Self.* London: Vision Press.

Herbert, G. (1593–1632). Employment; Frailty; Discipline; The Quip. In: *The Oxford Book of Christian Verse.* Oxford: Oxford University Press.

Hilton, W. (fourteenth century). *The Ladder of Perfection.* L. Shirley Price (Ed./Trans.). Harmondsworth: Penguin Classics.

Hopkins, G. M. (1844–1889) [1953]. J. Reeves (Ed.), *Selected Poems.* London: Heinemann.

Isaacs, S. (1948) [1952]. The nature and function of phantasy. In: M. Klein (Ed.), *Developments in Psychoanalysis.* London: Hogarth Press.

Jones, E. (1916) [1948]. The theory of symbolism. In: *Papers on Psycho-Analysis* (5th edn), London: Bailliere.

Julian of Norwich (fourteenth century mystic). *Revelations of Divine Love*. H. Blackhouse (Ed., with R. Pipe). London: Hodder & Stoughton.

Jung, C. G. (1954). *The Practise of Psychotherapy, C.W., 16*. London: Routledge.

Jung, C. G. (1958). *Psychology and Religion: West and East, C.W., 11*. London: Routledge & Kegan Paul.

Jung, C. G. (1960). *The Structure and Dynamics of the Psyche, C.W., 8*. London: Routledge.

Jung, C. G. (1971). *Memories,Dreams, Reflections*. London: Collins/ Routledge.

Kernberg, O. (1984). *Severe Personality Disorders*. Newhaven & London: Yale University Press.

Klein, J. (1995). *Doubts and Uncertainties in the Practice of Psychotherapy*. London: Karnac.

Klein, M. (1930) [1975]. The importance of symbol-formation in the development of the ego. In: *Collected Works of Melanie Klein*, Volume I, *Love, Guilt and Reparation, and Other Works* (pp. 219–232). London: Hogarth Press & Institute of Psychoanalysis [reprinted London: Virago, 1988].

Klein, M. (1945) [1975]. The Oedipus complex in the light of early anxieties. In: *Collected Works of Melanie Klein*, Volume I, *Love, Guilt and Reparation, and Other Works*. London: Hogarth Press & Institute of Psychoanalysis.

Klein, M. (1957). *Envy and Gratitude*. London: Hogarth Press [reprinted London: Virago, 1988].

Kohut, H. (1977). *The Restoration of the Self*. New York: International Universities Press.

Law, W. (1728 [1966]). *A Serious Call to a Devout and Holy Life*. London: Wyvern.

Little, M. (1986). On basic unity. In: *Transference Neurosis and Transference Psychosis: Towards Basic Unity*. London: Free Association Books.

Meltzer, D. (1967). Identification and socialisation in adolescence. *Contemporary Psychoanalysis*, 3:96. [Published in *Sexual States of Mind*. Strath Tay, Perthshire: The Clunie Press. 1973]

Meltzer, D. (1967). *The Psychoanalytical Process*. Strath Tay, Perthshire: The Clunie Press.

Meltzer, D. (1975). *Explorations in Autism*. Strath Tay: The Clunie Press.

Meltzer, D. (1979) [1973]. The introjective basis of polymorphous tendencies in adult sexuality. In: *Sexual States of Mind* (p. 78). Strath Tay, Perthshire: The Clunie Press.

Meltzer, D. (1988). *The Apprehension of Beauty*. Strath Tay: The Clunie Press

Meltzer, D. & Harris Williams, M. (1988) [1973]. *The Apprehension of Beauty. The Role of the Aesthetic Conflict in Development, Art and Violence*. Strath Tay, Perthshire: The Clunie Press.

Milner, M. (1952). Aspects of symbolism in comprehension of the not-self. (Later titled: Psycho-analytic concepts of the two functions of the symbol). *International Journal of Psycho-Analysis, 33*: 181–194.

Money-Kyrle, R. (1978) [1971]. The aim of psychoanalysis. In: D. Meltzer, (Ed.) *The Collected Papers of Roger Money-Kyrle*. Strath Tay, Pershire: The Clunie Press.

Ogden, T. H. (1992). *The Primitive Edge of Experience*. London: Karnac.

Proner, B. (1986). Defences of the self and envy of oneself [Michael Fordham reviewed]. *Journal of Analytical Psychology, 31*: 275–279.

Psychology (Makers of Modern Psychotherapy). London: Routledge.

Rose, G. (1987). Trauma and mastery in life and art. Yale. pp. 211–212. Quoted in Rose, G. (1991). Abstract art and emotion: expressive form and the sense of wholeness. *Journal of the American Psychoanalytic Association, 39*: 131–156.

Rosenfeld, H. (1971). A clinical approach to the psychoanalytic theory of the life and death instincts: an investigation into the aggressive aspects of narcissism. *International Journal of Psycho-analysis, 52*: 169–178. [Published in *Impasse and Interpretation*. London: Tavistock Publications, 1987].

Searles, H. (1965). Oedipal love in the countertransference. *Collected Papers on Schizophrenia*. New York: International Universities Press.

Segal, Hanna (1991). *Dream, Phantasy and Art*. London: Routledge/Tavistock.

St Francis of Assisi (1181–1226) [1926]. *The Little Flowers of St. Francis of Assisi*. Dom Roger Huddleston (Trans.) London: Burnes Oates and Washbourne Ltd.

Steiner, J. (1993). The relationship to reality in psychic retreats. In: J. Steiner, *Psychic Retreats*. London; Routledge.

Stern, D. et al (1998). Non-interpretative mechanisms in psychoanalytic therapy. *International Journal of Psycho-analysis, 79*: 903.

Tersteegen, G. (1918). *The Way of the Servant*. London: Watkins [reprinted Norwich: Pelegrine Trust in association with Pilgrim Books, 1987].

Tustin, F. (1992). *Autistic States in Children*. London: Routledge & Kegan Paul.

Tzu, Lao, (1963) [traditionally, first millennium BC] *Tao Te Ching*. D. C. Lau (Trans.). London: Penguin Books.

Vaughan, H. (1622–1695) [1940]. The Dawning. In: D. Cecil (Ed.), *The Oxford Book of Christian Verse*. Oxford: Oxford University Press.

Weber, M. (1908).Wirtschaft and Gesellschaft. In: H. H. Gerth & C. Wright Mills (Eds.) *From Max Weber: Essays in Sociology*. London: Routledge & Kegan Paul.

Weil, S. (1950). *Attente de Dieu (Waiting on God)*. London: Routledge & Kegan Paul.

Wilber, K. (1999). *One Taste*. Boston: Shambhala.

Williams, C. (1943). *The Figure of Beatrice*. Woodbridge, UK and Rochester, USA: Boydell and Brewer [re-issued by D. S. Brewer, 1994].

Williams, G. (1997). *Internal Landscapes and Foreign Bodies* (Tavistock Clinic Series). London: Gerald Duckworth.

Williams, G. (2000). Reflections on "aesthetic reciprocity". In: M. Cohen & A. Hahn (Eds.), *Exploring the Work of Donald Meltzer. A Festschrift* (pp. 136–151). London: Karnac.

Winnicott, D. W. (1965) [1963]. The development of the capacity for concern. In: *The Maturational Processes and the Facilitating Environment* (p. 73). London: Hogarth Press.

Winnicott, D. W. (1971). *Playing and Reality*. London: Tavistock [reprinted London: Penguin, 1974].

Wordsworth, W. (1876). In: A. B. Grosart (Ed.), *The Prose Works of Wm. Wordsworth. Vol. 2.* (p. 36). London: Edward Moxon.

INDEX